SCHOLASTIC

POP-UP Activities to Teach Genre

by Tamara B. Miller

NEW YORK • TORONTO • LONDON • AUCKLAND • SYDNEY
MEXICO CITY • NEW DELHI • HONG KONG • BUENOS AIRES

Teaching *Resources*

This book is dedicated to

First and foremost, my supportive and wonderful husband, Perry, and my daughter, Laurel; my literary and loving parents, Rose and August; and my diversely creative family, Mildred and Lothar, Helen, David, Dylan, Sela, Michael, Sharon, Aaron, Stephanie and Myles, Sylvia, and Chet.

True and supportive friends, because of whom life is joyous and good (in alphabetical order): Cyndi, Debbie, Elizabeth, Ellie, Fran, Gail, Julie, Judith, Larry, Maru, Rebecca, Roberta, Robin, and Swati.

Perry Miller, Roberta Gibson, and Fran Chandran for editing, babysitting, and celebrating.

I wish to acknowledge and thank the following sources for their assistance

The excellent and patient reference librarians at the Chandler Sunset Library:
Joe Schallan, Fran Wendtland, Nancy Weir, Janice Corker, Lisa Cooper, Debe Moreno, Jeremy Atkin, and Ezra Sitea. Special thanks to Marj Pals.

Emma L. Powers and Juliegh Clark of The Williamsburg Foundation for their information.

Lee Kreutzer at the National Trails Systems Office, Salt Lake City National Park Service. Peggy M. Baker, Director and Librarian at the Pilgrim Hall.

Finally, thank you to the following teachers who spent time editing or piloting these pages in their classrooms: Amy Wurtz, Kyrene Elementary School District; Lori Leggett, Janelle Yoder, and Monica Zepeda, Alhambra School District; Debbie Estrada Wolfram, homeschool representative. Special thanks to Tanner Wolfram and Laura Shwarz.

Cover design by Jason Robinson

Cover photographs by Studio 10

Cover and interior illustrations by George Ulrich

Interior design by Sydney Wright

Genre introduction pages edited by Betsy Yarbrough

ISBN: 0-439-45335-6

Copyright © 2005 by Tamara B. Miller

Published by Scholastic Inc.

All rights reserved.

Printed in the U.S.A.

1 2 3 4 5 6 7 8 9 10 40 13 12 11 10 09 08 07 06 05

CONTENTS

Introduction

Welcome to *Pop-Up Activities to Teach Genre*—a collection of super-engaging activities that help students write in nine different genres and create unique 3-D projects to showcase their stories. Students begin by using writing prompts and graphic organizers to help them generate ideas for their stories—mysteries, tall tales, adventure stories, personal narratives, and more. Then they use easy-to-assemble templates to create pop-up projects to illustrate their stories. These eye-catching projects are fun to create and fun to share. Students will enjoy reading each other's completed work as they pull tabs and lift flaps to reveal information unique to each student's story.

In this book, you'll find two writing activities for each of the following genres:

- ◉ Mystery
- ◉ Humorous fiction
- ◉ Science fiction
- ◉ Tall tales
- ◉ Fairy tales
- ◉ Historical fiction
- ◉ Personal narrative
- ◉ Expository writing
- ◉ Adventure

An introduction page is included for each genre with a description of the genre, two or more suggested books to share with students to provide a model of the genre, and teaching tips for helping students grasp the characteristics of the genre. The writing activities include the following elements:

Story Starter: Each writing activity begins with a read-aloud paragraph that describes the premise of the story students will write. These starters are designed to lead students into their stories, help them generate ideas, and motivate them to write.

Prewriting Page: These visually appealing reproducible graphic organizers help students generate and organize key information that they will use in their stories. These pages emphasize the importance of prewriting, help students brainstorm ideas, and give them direction for the writing process. Each prewriting page also includes a writing prompt that students can use or adapt for the first line of their stories.

Pop-Up Page: The pop-up pages are the reproducible templates for creating the 3-D projects that illustrate students' stories. Once students have drafted, revised, and edited their stories and are ready to write the final copy, they copy the beginning of their stories on the lines at the bottom of the pop-up page. Students then customize the illustration on the pop-up page to show a part of their stories. These pages often include an interactive element—such as flaps to lift or pieces to slide—that motivate students to create and share their projects.

Cutouts: Students use the cutouts to create the pop-up projects. Step-by-step directions on these pages explain how to construct the projects.

The writing activities in this book are designed to help students learn about genre in a highly engaging and memorable way. They provide students with the support they need to write in different genres and encourage them to follow the steps of the writing process. Students will have so much fun writing and illustrating their stories with pop-up projects that they won't even realize they are practicing and learning essential skills!

Connections to the Language Arts Standards

The activities in this book are designed to support you in meeting the following language arts standards for students in grades 3–5, outlined by Mid-continent Research for Education and Learning (McREL), an organization that collects and synthesizes national and state K–12 curriculum standards.

Writing

⑨ Uses the general skills and strategies of the writing process

— Uses prewriting strategies to plan written work (e.g., uses graphic organizers, story maps, and webs; groups related ideas; takes notes; brainstorms ideas; organizes information according to type and purpose of writing)

— Uses strategies to draft and revise written work

— Uses strategies to edit and publish written work

— Evaluates own and others' writing

— Uses strategies to write for a variety of purposes (e.g., to inform, entertain, explain, describe, record ideas)

— Writes expository compositions (e.g., identifies and stays on topic; develops the topic with simple facts, details, examples, and explanations; provides a concluding statement)

— Writes narrative accounts, such as poems and stories (e.g., establishes a context that enables the reader to imagine the event or experience; develops characters, setting, and plot; creates an organizing structure; sequences events)

— Writes autobiographical compositions (e.g., provides a context within which the incident occurs, uses simple narrative strategies, and provides some insight into why this incident was memorable)

⑨ Uses the stylistic and rhetorical aspects of writing

⑨ Uses grammatical and mechanical conventions in written compositions

⑨ Gathers and uses information for research purposes

Reading

⑨ Uses reading skills and strategies to understand and interpret a variety of literary texts (e.g., fiction, nonfiction, autobiographies, science fiction, tall tales)

— Knows the defining characteristics of a variety of literary forms and genres

Source: *Content Knowledge: A Compendium of Standards and Benchmarks for K–12 Education*, 4th edition (Mid-continent Research for Education and Learning, 2004)

How to Use This Book

This section describes in detail how to introduce the writing activities and guide students through the process of writing and creating their pop-up projects.

Introducing the Genre

Begin each writing activity by defining the genre for students. (Information is provided on each genre introduction page.) Start by asking students what they know about the genre and recording their ideas. Supplement the list to provide a complete definition. Ask students to think about books they have read or

books you have read together as a class that are of this genre. Select a book to read aloud to provide a model of the genre. Suggestions are provided on the genre introduction page. If time is limited and you are using a longer book, read aloud a few parts of the book that show some of the characteristics of the genre. On the genre introduction page, you'll find teaching tips for helping students grasp the characteristics of each genre.

Introducing the Activity

Each writing activity begins with a teacher page that provides a list of supplies, steps for guiding students through the activity,

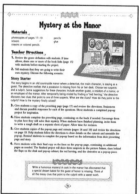

a read-aloud story starter, a photo of a sample pop-up project, and an extension activity. In advance, gather supplies and review the information on this page. Explain that each student will be writing a story in the genre you discussed and creating a pop-up project to illustrate a part of the story. Read aloud the story starter.

Prewriting

Give each student a copy of the prewriting page and review the directions together. Brainstorm and discuss possible responses for each of the questions. If students need additional room, have

them write on the backs of the pages or on extra sheets of paper. Encourage them to plan the beginning, middle, and ending of their stories. Show students a completed pop-up project for inspiration. You might have students discuss their prewriting sheets with a partner before writing their stories. Encourage partners to ask each other questions about their stories and provide constructive feedback.

Writing

On a separate sheet of paper, have students write their rough drafts. Remind them to use the information on their prewriting sheets. Explain to students that they may choose to use the writing prompt at the top of the prewriting page as the first line of their stories. Students may also adapt the prompt or write their own first lines.

Revising and Editing

Allow time for students to revise their rough drafts. You might have students work with a partner for this part of the process. Encourage students to read each other's stories and respond with thoughtful questions and suggestions. Provide them with a copy of the revision checklist on page 9. Have students edit their stories before they write their final drafts. Provide copies of the editing checklist on page 10 to guide the process.

Creating the Pop-Up Project

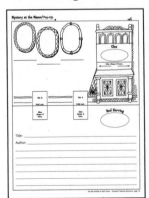
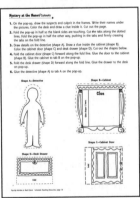

When students are ready to write their final copy, give them each a copy of the pop-up page and the cutouts page. Review the directions at the top of the cutouts page. Model the assembly steps for students and show them the completed project again. Remind students to complete their pop-ups based on information from their stories. Share the assembly tips below with students. Have students copy their final drafts on the lines on the pop-up page, continuing on as many additional sheets of paper as needed. (Provide copies of the lined paper on page 14.) Review the directions on page 8 for attaching additional pages and a cover.

Assessment

Give each student a copy of the self-assessment rubric on page 11. It is a good idea to give students the rubric before they begin the project so that they are clear about expectations and guidelines. When students have completed their projects, have them fill out the rubric. Use the assessment rubric on page 12 to evaluate students' work and provide feedback.

Assembly Tips

๏ Have students follow the directions on the cutout sheet. As the order of the directions indicates, it is easier to color the pop-up before cutting the pop-up tabs. It is also easier to draw details on the cutouts before cutting them out. Attach the cutout pieces to the pop-up page last.

๏ To prepare the tabs on the pop-up page, first cut along the solid black line around the outside of the pop-up page. Then fold the pop-up page in half, folding back along the solid fold line so the blank sides are touching. Cut the tab(s) along the dotted lines. As you refold the pop-up page in half the other way, gently push the tab(s) forward. If

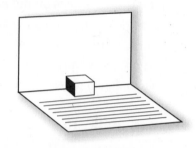

there are two tabs, push them forward one at a time. Then crease the tab(s) firmly on the fold line by pressing through the paper.

☺ When preparing the cutout pieces, cut along the dotted lines and fold along the solid fold lines. The directions specify whether to fold forward or back along the fold lines. If the directions call for folding forward, it is often easier first to fold back and then fold forward along the line. This allows you to see the fold line when making the initial fold.

☺ When gluing cutout pieces onto the pop-up pages, look for directions on the pop-up page indicating where to glue.

Attaching a Cover

To make the projects more durable, attach a cover. Fold a sheet of 9- by 12-inch construction paper in half widthwise so that the folded piece measures 9 by 6 inches. Spread a thin line of glue around the back of the top half of the completed pop-up page, without gluing the tabs. Place it in the cover, matching fold line to fold line. Then glue the bottom half of the pop-up page to the bottom half of the cover.

Adding Additional Pages

If students need additional writing paper, provide copies of page 14. Cut along the solid line around the outside of the additional writing page(s). Then fold the page(s) in half so the blank side is facing out. Stack the folded pages in order from top to bottom. When attaching the cover, glue only the top half of the pop-up to the folded construction paper. Place the folded additional page(s) beneath the pop-up page. Glue the top half of the first additional writing page to the bottom half of the pop-up page, lining up the corners and fold lines. Then

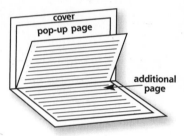

glue the blank sides of the additional pages together. Finally, glue the bottom of the last additional page to the bottom half of the cover.

Independent Writing Center

Place the following materials in a center:

- photocopies of the blank pop-up template on page 13
- unlined 8½- by 11-inch white paper, cut into quarters
- 9- by 12-inch construction paper
- scissors, glue, pencils, and crayons or markers

Explain to students that they will write a story in any genre they choose. They will then use the templates and other supplies to design their own pop-up projects. Demonstrate how to cut a tab and attach a pop-up piece. Review how to attach additional pages and add a construction paper cover. In addition to writing stories, students can also use the pop-up template to create letters, invitations, greeting cards, pop-up poems, and more.

Revision Checklist

Author's Name _____ Date _____

Title _____ Genre _____

Revision Partner's Name _____

Partner's Feedback

1. ☐ I read my partner's story.

2. ☐ I drew stars by parts that were strong. I explained to my partner why I marked these sections.
I marked _____ with a star because

_____

_____

_____

3. ☐ I drew arrows by parts that could be improved. I explained to my partner why I marked
these sections. I marked _____ with an arrow because

_____

_____

_____

4. ☐ I circled words that could be replaced with stronger words.

5. ☐ I asked my partner questions about the story. Here's a question I asked:

_____

Author's Revision

1. ☐ I reread my story.

2. ☐ I used my partner's feedback to revise my story. These are some of the changes I made:

a. _____

b. _____

c. _____

3. ☐ I replaced weaker words with stronger, more specific words. These are some of the words
I replaced.

	Old Word	New Word
a.	_____	_____
b.	_____	_____
c.	_____	_____

Editing Checklist

Name _____ Date _____

Title _____ Genre _____

1. ☐ I wrote in complete sentences.

2. ☐ I used correct punctuation.

3. ☐ I capitalized the first words of sentences, names, and appropriate words in titles.

4. ☐ I corrected spelling mistakes.

5. ☐ I grouped ideas into paragraphs and indented each new paragraph.

- -

Editing Checklist

Name _____ Date _____

Title _____ Genre _____

1. ☐ I wrote in complete sentences.

2. ☐ I used correct punctuation.

3. ☐ I capitalized the first words of sentences, names, and appropriate words in titles.

4. ☐ I corrected spelling mistakes.

5. ☐ I grouped ideas into paragraphs and indented each new paragraph.

Self-Assessment Rubric

Name _____ Date _____

Title _____ Genre _____

Mark each sentence with a score.
3 Excellent
2 Good
1 Needs improvement

Content

1. The piece is fully developed with details, examples, or descriptions. _____

2. The sequence of events or ideas make sense. _____

3. The piece has a beginning, middle, and ending. _____

4. The writing is strong and lively. _____

5. The beginning grabs the reader's attention. _____

6. The ending is satisfying and wraps up the piece. _____

Editing

1. I spelled all or most of the words correctly. _____

2. I used appropriate punctuation and capitalization. _____

3. I wrote in complete sentences and avoided run-on sentences. _____

4. I grouped ideas into paragraphs and indented new paragraphs. _____

Presentation

1. My handwriting is neat and legible. _____

2. The pop-up project is colorful, appealing, and neatly assembled. _____

Comments _____

_____

_____

_____

_____

_____

Assessment Rubric

Student _____ Date _____

Title _____ Genre _____

3	Excellent
2	Satisfactory
1	Needs improvement

Content

1. The topic is fully developed. Relevant details, examples, and descriptions clarify and enhance ideas. _____

2. The sequence of events or ideas makes sense. The piece has an engaging introduction, a well-developed middle, and a satisfying conclusion. _____

3. The writing is strong and lively. It includes active verbs, specific nouns, and vivid descriptions. _____

4. For fictional stories: Characters are well developed. _____

5. For expository writing and historical fiction: The student's research is evident. Rich, accurate details are incorporated into the piece. _____

Editing

1. Spelling, punctuation, and capitalization are generally correct. _____

2. Sentences are complete and do not include run-ons. _____

3. Ideas are grouped into paragraphs and new paragraphs are indented. _____

Presentation

1. Handwriting is neat and legible. _____

2. The pop-up project is colorful, appealing, and neatly assembled. The illustration has thoughtfully represented a part of the story. _____

Comments _____

_____

_____

Pop-Up Template

Title: _____

Author: _____

_____

_____

_____

_____

_____

_____

Lined Paper

MYSTERY

About the Genre

Solving a mystery is like piecing together a puzzle to reveal the whole picture. The story often evolves from a crime that has been committed or a problem that needs to be solved. This type of mystery usually includes a detective who solves the mystery through deductive reasoning. There is a cast of suspects, each of whom must have a motive and opportunity for committing the crime. One of the suspects, the actual culprit, often leaves behind visible clues. There may also be a "red herring"— a piece of evidence that does not lead to the culprit and temporarily misleads the readers and detective. The story culminates with the revelation of the culprit—hence, the term *whodunits*. Many mystery writers have written series of books, allowing readers to follow favorite detectives and their endearing sidekicks through a multitude of adventures.

Book Links

Encyclopedia Brown, Boy Detective
by Donald J. Sobol (T. Nelson, 1963)
In the first book of this popular series, we meet Encyclopedia Brown—a fifth-grade genius who assists the Idaville police. Each book encourages readers to try to solve the cases as they read, and all solutions are included in the back.

From the Mixed-Up Files of Mrs. Basil E. Frankweiler
by E. L. Koningsburg (Atheneum, 1967)
In this Newbery Medal winner, two siblings run away from home to live in a New York museum and end up involved in a mystery.

Teaching Tips

✳ Discuss the characteristics of mysteries. Present the terms that are associated with mysteries, such as *clue*, *suspect*, *alibi*, *deduction*, *evidence*, *red herring*, *sleuth*, and *witness*.

✳ Read a mystery aloud and have students search for clues, evidence, suspects, red herrings, and so on. Decorate a bulletin board with large, simple shapes, such as magnifying glasses or thumbprints. Label each shape with a term, such as *clue* and *suspect*. Invite students to fill in the shapes with information as it is revealed in the book.

✳ Discuss the type of mood that mystery writers often portray. Ask students to think of ways that authors accomplish this. What type of language do they use? How does the setting of the story affect the mood? Challenge students to write a descriptive paragraph conveying a specific mood. Then encourage students to consider the mood they would like to create in their mystery.

Mystery at the Manor

Materials

photocopies of pages 17–19   pencils
scissors   glue
crayons or colored pencils

Teacher Directions

1. Review the genre definition with students. If time allows, share one or more of the book links (page 15) with students before starting the project.

2. Tell students that they are going to write their own mystery. Discuss the following scenario:

Story Starter

The story begins in an old countryside manor where a detective, the main character, is staying as a guest. The detective realizes that a possession is missing from his or her desk. Choose two suspects and a culprit. Some suggestions for these characters include another guest, a resident of the manor, or an employee of the manor. After temporarily being misled by finding a "red herring," the detective discovers two clues that point to one of three suspects. What are the clues? How do they point to the culprit? How is the mystery finally solved?

3. Give students a copy of the prewriting page (page 17) and review the directions. Brainstorm and discuss possible responses for each of the questions. Show students a completed pop-up project for inspiration.

4. Have students complete the prewriting page, continuing on the back if needed. Encourage them to plan how they will solve their mystery. When students have finished planning, invite them to write a rough draft on a separate sheet of paper. Allow time for revision.

5. Give students copies of the pop-up page and cutouts (pages 18 and 19) and review the directions on page 19. Help students follow the directions to draw details on the cutouts and assemble the pop-up. Remind students to complete the pop-up based on the information from their prewriting page and story.

6. Have students write their final copy on the lines on the pop-up page, continuing on additional pages as needed. The finished project will show three suspects in the picture frames, clues behind the flaps on the desk and pop-up cabinet, the red herring, and the detective as a pop-up piece.

Extension Activity

Write a humorous mystery! A cook in the manor has discovered that a special dessert baked for the guest of honor is missing. Think of all the messy clues that point to the culprit with a sweet tooth.

Name _____ Date _____

Mystery at the Manor

Complete this page to plan your mystery. You may use the prompt below to begin.

It was almost midnight. _____ retired to his/her
(main character)

drafty room at the _____ Manor.
(name of manor)

Main Character's Name:

_____

Describe the main character.

_____

_____

_____

_____

Missing Item: _____

Describe the missing item.

_____

_____

What are the two clues?

Clue #1: _____

_____

_____

Clue #2: _____

_____

_____

What is the red herring?

_____

_____

GALLERY OF SUSPECTS

Name:
_____

Motive: _____

_____

_____

Name:
_____

Motive: _____

_____

_____

Name:
_____

Motive: _____

_____

_____

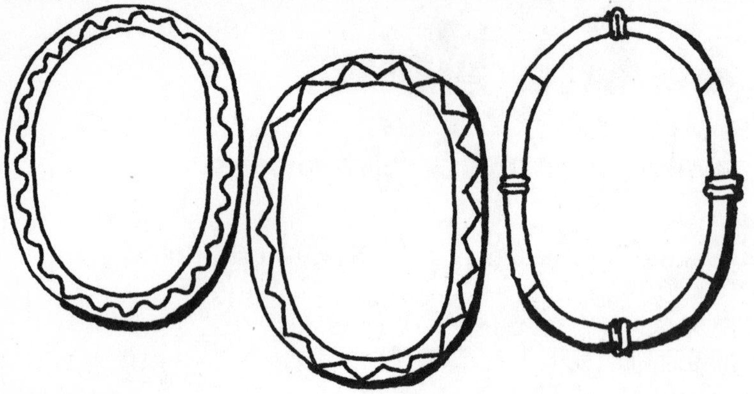

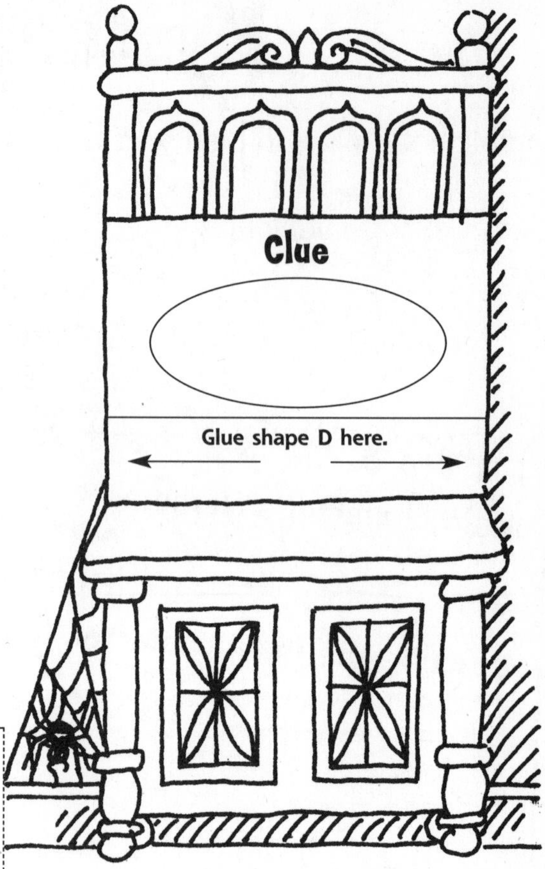

Clue

Glue shape D here.

Tab B

Fold out.

Glue shape B here.

Tab A

Fold out.

Glue shape A here.

Red Herring

Title: _____

Author: _____

_____

_____

_____

_____

_____

_____

1. On the pop-up, draw the suspects and culprit in the frames. Write their names under the pictures. Color the desk and draw a clue inside it. Cut out the page.

2. Fold the pop-up in half so the blank sides are touching. Cut the tabs along the dotted lines. Fold the pop-up in half the other way, pushing in the tabs and firmly creasing the tabs on the fold line.

3. Draw details on the detective (shape A). Draw a clue inside the cabinet (shape B). Color the cabinet door (shape C) and desk drawer (shape D). Cut out the shapes below.

4. Fold the cabinet door (shape C) forward along the fold line. Glue the door to the cabinet (shape B). Glue the cabinet to tab B on the pop-up.

5. Fold the desk drawer (shape D) forward along the fold line. Glue the drawer to the desk on pop-up.

6. Glue the detective (shape A) to tab A on the pop-up.

Shape A—Detective

Shape B—Cabinet

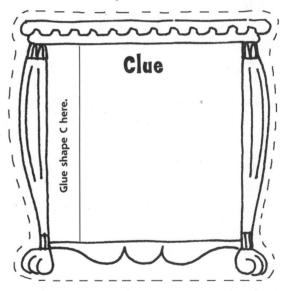

Shape C—Cabinet Door

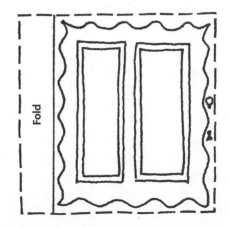

Shape D—Desk Drawer

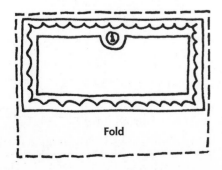

Mystery Under the Big Top

Materials

photocopies of pages 21–23   pencils
scissors   glue
crayons or colored pencils

Teacher Directions

1. Review the genre definition with students. If time allows, share one or more of the book links (page 15) with students before starting the project.

2. Tell students that they are going to write their own mystery. Discuss the following scenario:

Story Starter

The story begins under the tent at the Big Top Circus. The performers hurry to get ready for the show as the audience cheers in anticipation. Moments before the show is about to start, a prop or animal mysteriously disappears. The master of ceremonies announces that the show cannot go on until the mystery has been solved. Luckily, a famous detective is in the audience with his or her nephew or niece (a detective-in-training). After temporarily being misled by finding a "red herring," the detective discovers two clues that point to one of three suspects. What are the clues? How do they point to the culprit? How is the mystery finally solved?

3. Give students a copy of the prewriting page (page 21) and review the directions. Brainstorm and discuss possible responses for each of the questions. Show students a completed pop-up project for inspiration.

4. Have students complete the prewriting page, continuing on the back if needed. Encourage them to plan how they will solve their mystery. When students have finished planning, invite them to write a rough draft on a separate sheet of paper. Allow time for revision.

5. Give students copies of the pop-up page and cutouts (pages 22 and 23) and review the directions on page 23. Help students follow the directions to draw details on the cutouts and assemble the pop-up. Remind students to complete the pop-up based on the information from their prewriting page and story.

6. Have students write their final copy on the lines of the pop-up page, continuing on additional pages as needed. The finished project will show the culprit and two suspects, clues under the flaps on the tent, and the detective and red herring as a pop-up piece.

Extension Activity

Retell your mystery from the point of view of one of the suspects. You might describe the suspect's experience of being falsely accused and how the suspect convinced the detective that he or she was innocent. Write a surprise ending for this new twist on your mystery.

Name _____ Date _____

Mystery Under the Big Top

Complete this page to plan your mystery. You may use the prompt below to begin.

Ladies and gentlemen, welcome to the Big Top Circus! Unfortunately, tonight's performance has been canceled due to the mysterious disappearance of

_____. *Is there a detective in the house?*

(missing object or animal)

Detective's Name and Description:

_____

_____

Missing Object or Animal:

_____

_____

SUSPECTS

Name:

_____

Motive:

_____

_____

_____

Name:

_____

Motive:

_____

_____

_____

Name:

_____

Motive:

_____

_____

_____

Clue #1:

_____

_____

_____

Clue #2:

_____

_____

Red Herring:

_____

_____

Mystery Under the Big Top/ Pop-Up

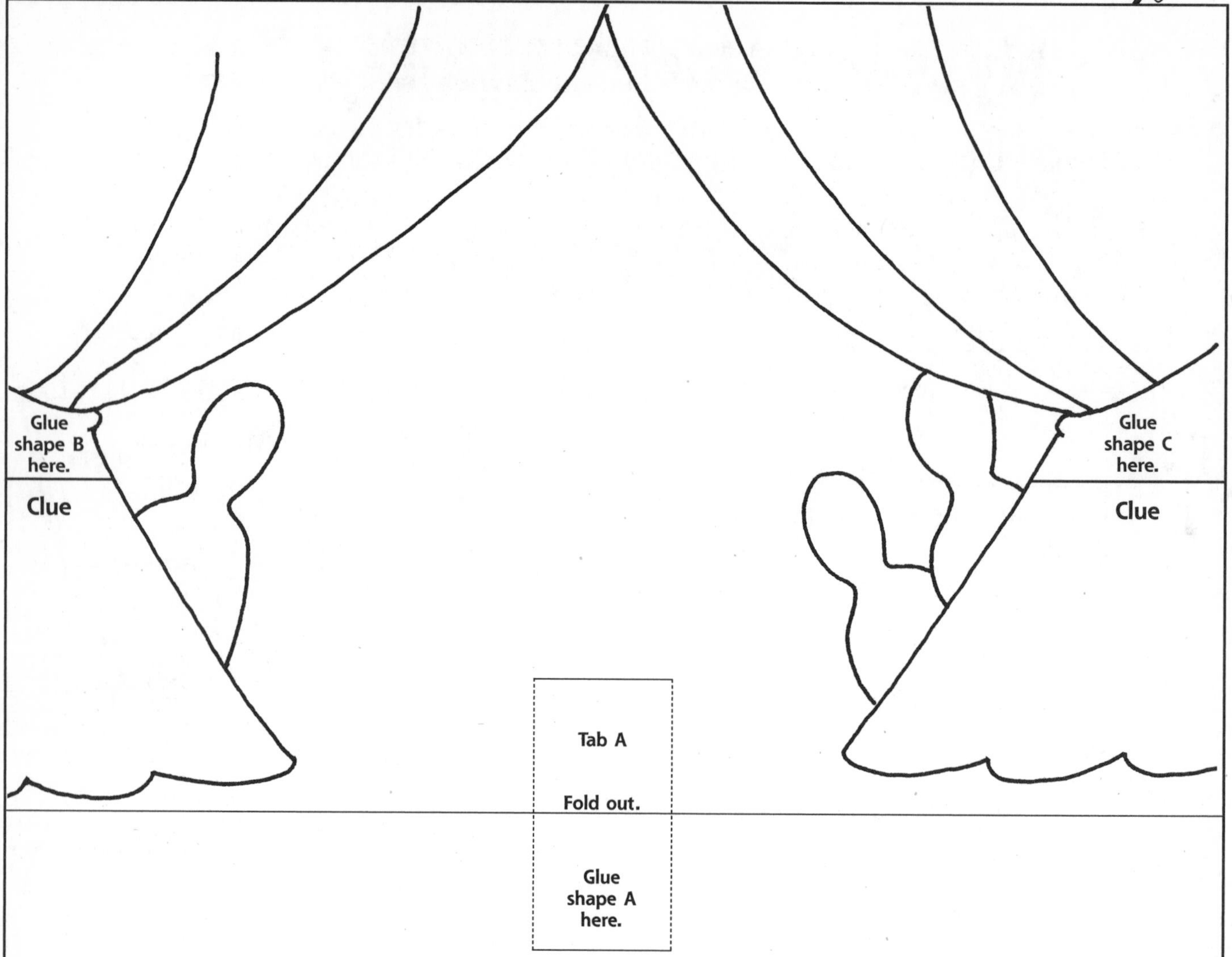
Glue shape B here.
Clue
Glue shape C here.
Clue
Tab A
Fold out.
Glue shape A here.

Title: ______________________________

Author: ______________________________

____

____

____

____

____

____

1. On the pop-up, draw clue #1 and clue #2 on the tent. Draw details on the two suspects and culprit. Color the illustrations and cut out the page.

2. Fold the pop-up in half so the blank sides are touching. Cut the tab along the dotted lines. Fold the pop-up in half the other way, pushing in the tab and firmly creasing the tab on the fold line.

3. Draw details on the detective (shape A) and draw the red herring on the pedestal. Color the tent flaps (shapes B and C). Cut out the shapes below.

4. Glue the detective (shape A) to tab A on the pop-up.

5. Fold the tent flaps (shapes B and C) forward along the fold lines. Glue the flaps to the pop-up.

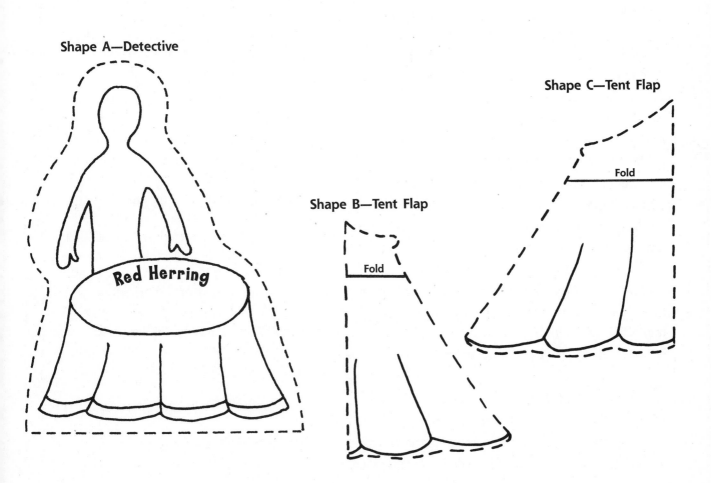

Shape A—Detective

Shape C—Tent Flap

Shape B—Tent Flap

Red Herring

Fold

Fold

HUMOROUS FICTION

About the Genre

In humorous fiction, the main purpose is to entertain and amuse the reader. Writers of this genre often create humor through continuous, unexpected events that surprise the reader and tickle the funny bone. Sometimes it is the surprising way that characters try to resolve their problems that creates a humorous situation. Other times, it is a misunderstanding that produces unexpected results. Some writers make us laugh with the clever details they include throughout their stories. Some writers remind us of humorous situations we have experienced ourselves. And other writers exaggerate a situation so that it doesn't resemble reality at all.

There are many different approaches to creating humor. Writers might appeal to the reader's intellect with witty jokes. Or they might describe a scene of physical comedy and antics. Puns create humor through creative play with language. Satire mocks a particular subject and parody creates humor through exaggerated imitation. Students may not have encountered all of these types of humor in their reading. Share examples of different types of humor that are appropriate for their age group. Compare humorous fiction to other genres that may include humor, such as personal narrative and tall tales.

Teaching Tips

* Review the characteristics of humorous fiction and the different types of humor students have encountered in books you have read together in class.

* Create a bulletin board for students to display humorous cartoons, quotations, or stories. Invite students to explain the elements of humor that apply to their selections.

* Invite student volunteers to tell a joke or share a funny tale. You might use some of these stories as a starting place for humorous fiction writing assignments.

* Create a collection of humorous fiction story starters. On index cards, write an unexpected event that could lead to a humorous tale, such as discovering your new neighbor has an unusual collection or getting lost on a trip and ending up in a surprising destination. Have students choose a story starter when they are stuck for ideas.

Book Links

Henry and Ribsy by Beverly Cleary (Morrow, 1954)
An uproarious story of a boy named Henry and his dog Ribsy. The more Henry does to keep Ribsy out of trouble, the deeper in trouble they both get.

The Day Jimmy's Boa Ate the Wash by Trinka Hakes Noble (Dial Press, 1980)
This read-aloud picture book perfectly illustrates continuous unexpected events leading up to a surprise happy ending. A class trip to a farm becomes riotous when a student's pet boa escapes on the premises.

Up a Tree

Materials

photocopies of pages 26–28   pencils
scissors   glue
crayons or colored pencils

Teacher Directions

1. Review the genre definition with students. If time allows, share one or more of the book links (page 24) with students before starting the project.

2. Tell students that they are going to write their own humorous story. Discuss the following scenario:

Story Starter

The story begins on a sunny spring day at the park. As the main character is taking his or her dog out for a walk, the character sees a neighbor with his or her pet enjoying a picnic lunch under a tree. The dog breaks free from its leash and chases the neighbor's pet around the tree and through the picnic lunch, creating a sticky mess! The pet rushes up the tree with the dog in hot pursuit. Continue the high-action sequence of events by describing several failed attempts to rescue the pet. How is the chaos finally resolved? How does the pet return safely to its owner?

3. Give students a copy of the prewriting page (page 26) and review the directions. Brainstorm and discuss possible responses for each of the questions. Show students a completed pop-up project for inspiration.

4. Have students complete the prewriting page, continuing on the back if needed. Encourage them to incorporate unexpected twists in their story. Do the characters do anything that makes the situation worse before it is resolved? When students have finished planning, invite them to write a rough draft on a separate sheet of paper. Allow time for revision.

5. Give students copies of the pop-up page and cutouts (pages 27 and 28) and review the directions on page 28. Help students follow the directions to draw details on the cutouts and assemble the pop-up. Remind students to complete the pop-up based on the information from their prewriting page and story.

6. Have students write their final copy on the lines of the pop-up page, continuing on additional pages as needed. The finished project will show the dog and its owner on a pop-up piece and the pet on a movable piece being chased up the tree.

Extension Activity

Rewrite the story as a dialogue between the two pets, who are actually engaged in a friendly game of chase. What are their observations of how their human companions react to their fun romp? Begin the dialogue from the moment the dog spies the neighbor's pet and invites it to play.

Name _____ Date _____

Up a Tree

Complete this page to plan your humorous story. You may use the prompt below to begin.

My dog _____ scampered in front of me through the park.
(dog's name)
Suddenly he spotted my neighbor _____ and began barking uncontrollably.
(neighbor's name)

Describe the dog chasing the pet up the tree.

_____
_____
_____
_____
_____

Describe the first unsuccessful rescue attempt.

_____
_____
_____
_____
_____

Describe the second unsuccessful rescue attempt.

_____
_____
_____
_____

Describe how the pet was finally rescued.

_____
_____
_____
_____

Main Character's Name:

_____

Dog's Name:

_____

Neighbor's Name:

_____

Kind of Pet: _____

Pet's Name: _____

Glue top of
shape A here.

Tab B

Fold out.

Glue
shape B
here.

Glue bottom of
shape A here.

Title: _____

Author: _____

_____

_____

_____

_____

_____

Up a Tree/Cutouts

1. On the pop-up, color the background. Cut out the page.

2. Fold the pop-up in half so the blank sides are touching. Cut the tab along the dotted lines. Fold the pop-up in half the other way, pushing in the tab and firmly creasing the tab on the fold line.

3. Color the tree trunk (shape A) and the treetop (shape C). Color the dog and draw details on the main character (shape B). Draw the neighbor's pet in a climbing position (shape D). Cut out the shapes below.

4. Fold the tree trunk (shape A) as shown. Glue the tree trunk to the boxes on the pop-up. Glue the treetop (shape C) to the top of the tree trunk.

5. Fold shape D back along the fold lines. Wrap the strip around the tree trunk. Then glue the end of the strip to the back of shape D with a small dab of glue. NOTE: Do not glue shape D to the tree trunk.

6. Glue the main character (shape B) to tab B on the pop-up.

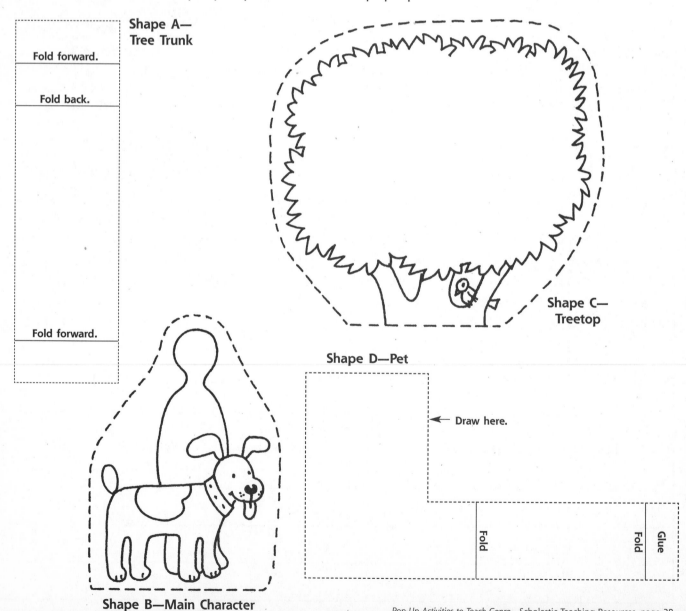

Shape A— Tree Trunk

Fold forward.

Fold back.

Fold forward.

Shape C— Treetop

Shape D—Pet

Draw here.

Fold

Fold

Glue

Shape B—Main Character

The Tale of the Naughty Kangaroo

Materials

photocopies of pages 30–32
scissors
crayons or colored pencils

pencils
glue

Teacher Directions

1. Review the genre definition with students. If time allows, share one or more of the book links (page 24) with students before starting the project.

2. Tell students that they are going to write their own humorous story. Discuss the following scenario:

Story Starter

The story takes place in the outback of Australia. The main character and his or her family have set up a tent for a weekend of camping amid baobab trees and kangaroos. One mischievous kangaroo manages to take something important belonging to one of the family members. The kangaroo stealthily hides the object inside her pouch. Why is the object important? How does the family react to the kangaroo's actions? Describe the series of humorous attempts to retrieve the object. In the end, is the family successful or not?

3. Give students a copy of the prewriting page (page 30) and review the directions. Brainstorm and discuss possible responses for each of the questions. Show students a completed pop-up project for inspiration.

4. Have students complete the prewriting page, continuing on the back if needed. Encourage them to plan the beginning, middle, and end of their stories. When students have finished planning, invite them to write a rough draft on a separate sheet of paper. Allow time for revision.

5. Give students copies of the pop-up page and cutouts (pages 31 and 32) and review the directions on page 32. Help students follow the directions to draw details on the cutouts and assemble the pop-up. Remind students to complete the pop-up based on the information from their prewriting page and story.

6. Have students write their final copy on the lines of the pop-up page, continuing on additional pages as needed. The finished project will show pop-up pieces of the main character and the kangaroo with the stolen object in its pouch.

Extension Activity

What other animals does the family encounter as they travel through Australia? Write a humorous story involving wombats, koala bears, kookaburras, bandicoots, echidnas, quolls, platypuses, emus, or even Tasmanian devils! First, do some research to find out about your animal and its habitat. Then write about how your creature causes trouble for the family as they try to enjoy their trip Down Under.

Name _____ Date _____

The Tale of the Naughty Kangaroo

Complete this page to plan your humorous story. You may use the prompt below to begin.

Crikey! A kangaroo took off with . . .

Name and describe the main character.

_____

_____

_____

_____

Missing Object:

_____

Why is this object important to the family?

_____

_____

_____

_____

_____

How do the characters attempt to retrieve the object?

First . . .

_____

_____

_____

_____

Next . . .

_____

_____

_____

_____

_____

Finally . . .

_____

_____

_____

_____

_____

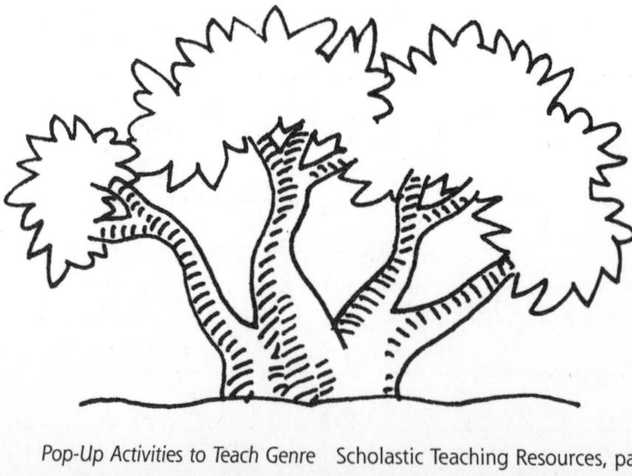

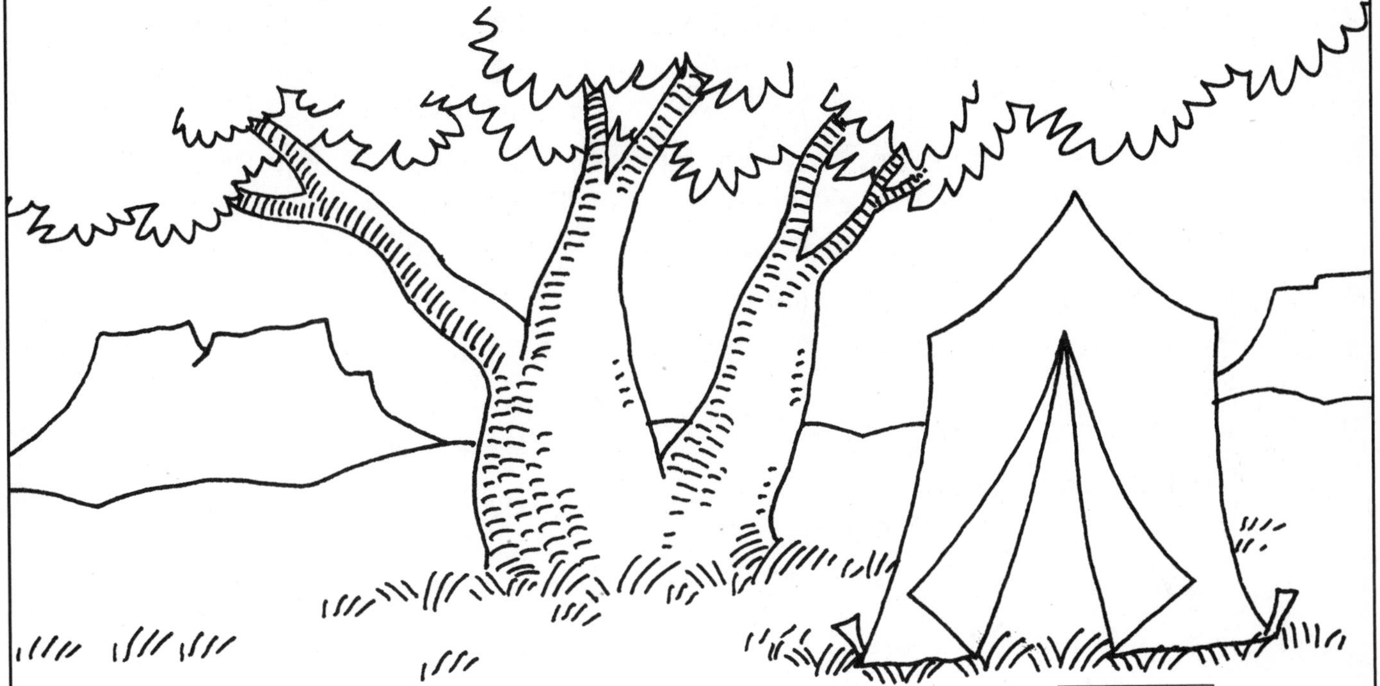

Tab A

Fold out.

Tab B

Fold out.

Glue
shape A
here.

Glue
shape B
here.

Title: _____

Author: _____

_____

_____

_____

_____

_____

_____

1. On the pop-up, color the baobab tree, tent, and background. Cut out the page.

2. Fold the pop-up in half so the blank sides are touching. Cut the tabs along the dotted lines. Fold the pop-up in half the other way, pushing in the tabs and firmly creasing the tabs on the fold line.

3. Color the kangaroo (shape A) and draw the stolen object in the center of its body. Color the pouch flap (shape C) the same color as the kangaroo. Draw details on the main character (shape B). Cut out the shapes below.

4. Fold shape C forward along the fold line. Glue shape C to the kangaroo (shape A).

5. Glue the kangaroo (shape A) to tab A on the pop-up. Glue the main character (shape B) to tab B.

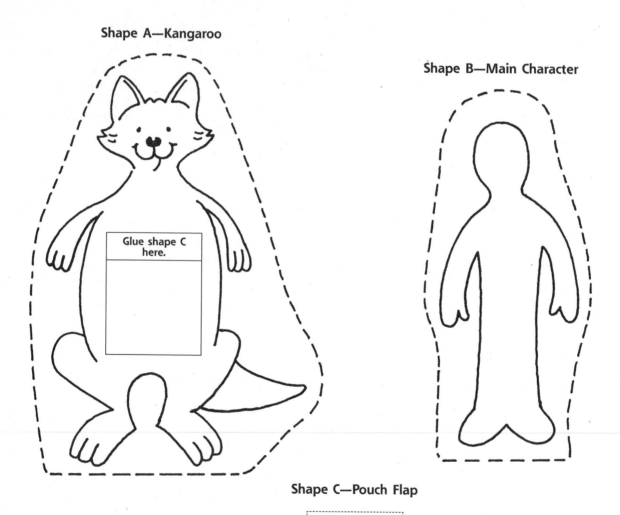

Shape A—Kangaroo

Glue shape C here.

Shape B—Main Character

Shape C—Pouch Flap

Glue

Fold

SCIENCE FICTION

About the Genre

Science fiction writers pair their imaginative ideas with thoroughly researched scientific data to explore the question "What if?" They write about events that could possibly happen based on scientific advancements that have already taken place. Science fiction stories may take place in the near or distant future, or they may explore what could have happened in the past. Science fiction differs from fantasy, in which anything can happen. Another distinction is that, unlike fantasy stories, magic plays no part in science fiction. The characters respond to problems in realistic ways that are built on what the author knows about scientific data.

Science fiction writers may use their stories as a vehicle to pose moral and ethical questions about the consequences of ecological or technological developments. In science fiction, a new technology often seems to be operating smoothly at first, but the main character soon becomes aware of a flaw or glitch that creates a dilemma for the characters in the story. These stories challenge the readers to consider these issues and think about what they would do in a situation that perhaps might occur in the future.

Book Links

Top Secret by John Reynolds Gardiner
(Little, Brown, 1984)
Allen Brewster has an amazing idea for his school science project: human photosynthesis—turning sunlight into food for humans. No one believes in his project until he himself turns suspiciously plantlike.

The Sorcerer's Apprentice by Ted Dewan
(Doubleday, 1998)
In this read-aloud picture book, an inventor creates a robot apprentice to clean up his workshop. The apprentice, in turn, contrives to create his own robotic helper. But his invention goes awry in this retelling of the classic Frankenstein tale.

Teaching Tips

* Review the characteristics of science fiction with students. Discuss science fiction books you have read together as a class and determine which characteristics of the genre they show.

* Have students search magazines, newspapers, or Web sites for stories about recent scientific discoveries and technological breakthroughs. Post student findings and have small groups consider how science fiction writers might use these new facts as springboards for stories.

* When reading examples of science fiction, such as the book links, review the story elements of setting, plot, and character. Remind students that these are part of science fiction as well.

The Wonder Vegetable

Materials

photocopies of pages 35–37
scissors
crayons or colored pencils

pencils
glue

Teacher Directions

1. Review the genre definition with students. If time allows, share one or more of the book links (page 33) with students before starting the project.

2. Tell students that they are going to write their own science fiction story. Discuss the following scenario:

Story Starter

The story begins in the main character's backyard on a sunny afternoon in the near future. For a school science experiment, this character has engineered a new and original type of vegetable that offers some great benefits that ordinary vegetables don't. However, the character soon notices that there is one major problem with this veggie. What is it? How does the character deal with this problem?

3. Give students a copy of the prewriting page (page 35) and review the directions. Brainstorm and discuss possible responses for each of the questions. Show students a completed pop-up project for inspiration.

4. Have students complete the prewriting page, continuing on the back if needed. Encourage students to plan how the character will resolve the problem with the vegetable, reminding them that the character should act in a believable way. When students have finished planning, invite them to write a rough draft on a separate sheet of paper. Allow time for revision.

5. Give students copies of the pop-up page and cutouts (pages 36 and 37) and review the directions on page 37. Help students follow the directions to draw details on the cutout and assemble the pop-up. Remind students to complete the pop-up based on the information from their prewriting page and story.

6. Have students write their final copy on the lines of the pop-up page, continuing on additional pages as needed. The finished project will show the main character with a watering can and a crop of the invented vegetables on a pop-up piece. (Students may create their own pop-up piece showing the vegetable growing on a vine, tree, or another type of plant.)

Extension Activity

Write a tale of another invention gone awry. Imagine that your character has invented a new kind of product designed to improve one's quality of life. Unfortunately, this product has one major flaw. What is it and what kind of problems does it cause? How does the character react? What does he or she finally decide to do about the invention?

Name _____ Date _____

The Wonder Vegetable

Complete this page to plan your science fiction story. You may use the prompt below to begin.

Finally, my _____ *was ripe and ready to be picked!*
(name of invented vegetable)

Character's Name:
_____

Describe the main character.
_____
_____
_____
_____

Describe the invented vegetable.
_____
_____
_____
_____

Describe the benefits of the vegetable.
_____
_____
_____

Describe the problem with the vegetable.
_____
_____
_____

How does the character respond to the problem?
_____
_____
_____
_____

Tab A

Fold out.

Glue
shape A
here.

Title: _____

Author: _____

_____

_____

_____

_____

_____

_____

The Wonder Vegetable/Cutouts

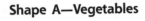

1. On the pop-up, draw details on the main character. Color the background and cut out the page.

2. Fold the pop-up in half so the blank sides are touching. Cut the tab along the dotted lines. Fold the pop-up in half the other way, pushing in the tab and firmly creasing the tab on the fold line.

3. Draw the vegetable from your story growing from the stalks (shape A). Cut out shape A.

4. Glue the vegetables (shape A) to tab A on the pop-up.

Shape A—Vegetables

It's a Robot's Life

Materials

photocopies of pages 39–41
scissors
crayons or colored pencils

pencils
glue

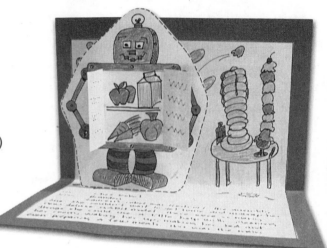

Teacher Directions

1. Review the genre definition with students. If time allows, share one or more of the book links (page 33) with students before starting the project.

2. Tell students that they are going to write their own science fiction story. Discuss the following scenario:

Story Starter

The story begins in the main character's house sometime in the near future. The main character has purchased a robot to help him or her perform various tasks. One day, a major flaw in the robot's circuitry becomes apparent, causing chaos for the main character. What is the robot's flaw and what trouble does it cause? How does the main character resolve this problem?

3. Give students a copy of the prewriting page (page 39) and review the directions. Brainstorm and discuss possible responses for each of the questions. Show students a completed pop-up project for inspiration.

4. Have students complete the prewriting page, continuing on the back if needed. Encourage students to plan the conclusion of their story, keeping in mind that the characters should act in realistic ways. When students have finished planning, invite them to write a rough draft on a separate sheet of paper. Allow time for revision.

5. Give students copies of the pop-up page and cutouts (pages 40 and 41) and review the directions on page 41. Help students follow the directions to draw details on the cutouts and assemble the pop-up. Remind students to complete the pop-up based on the information from their prewriting page and story.

6. Have students write their final copy on the lines of the pop-up page, continuing on additional pages as needed. The finished project will show a large pop-up robot in an exciting scene from the story. Beneath the flaps, students draw objects that relate to the tasks the robot can perform or that relate to other aspects of their story.

Extension Activity

Rewrite the story, changing the bad flaw into a surprising positive feature. How does this change the story? Do you think it is as interesting? Does it grab the reader's attention as much as the original story? Why or why not?

Name _____ Date _____

It's a Robot's Life

Complete this page to plan your science fiction story. You may use the prompt below to begin.

_____ 's robot was fresh off the assembly line.
(main character)

Robot

What does it look like?

_____

_____

_____

_____

_____

What can it do?

_____

_____

_____

_____

_____

What is its flaw?

_____

_____

_____

_____

Main Character

Name and Description:

_____

_____

_____

Problem

What problems occur because of the robot's flaw?

_____

_____

_____

_____

How does the main character respond to the problems?

_____

_____

_____

_____

Tab A

Fold out.

Glue shape A here.

Title: _____

Author: _____

_____

_____

_____

_____

_____

It's a Robot's Life/Cutouts

1. On the pop-up, draw an exciting event from your story. You may want to include the main character and other characters. Cut out the page.

2. Fold the pop-up in half so the blank sides are touching. Cut the tab along the dotted lines. Fold the pop-up in half the other way, pushing in the tab and firmly creasing the tab on the fold line.

3. Draw details on the robot (shape A). Draw objects or tools that the robot uses in its center area that will be covered with flaps (shapes B and C). Cut out the shapes below.

4. Fold shapes B and C forward along the fold lines. Glue shapes B and C to the center of the robot. Draw details on the flaps.

5. Glue the robot (shape A) to tab A on the pop-up.

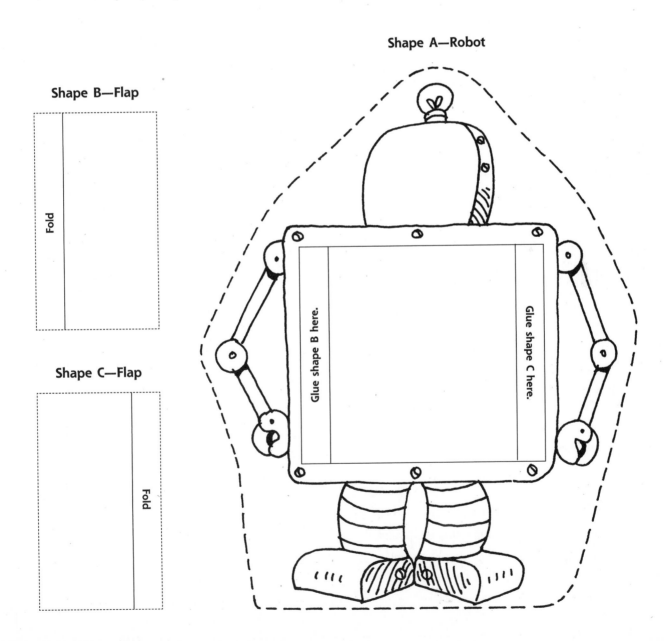

Shape A—Robot

Shape B—Flap

Fold

Shape C—Flap

Fold

Glue shape B here.

Glue shape C here.

TALL TALES

About the Genre

The tall tale originated in North America as pioneers tackled the challenges of the untamed frontier. In order to survive, these early settlers needed to be resourceful, hardworking, courageous, and clever. The heroes and heroines of tall tales embody these same qualities, although in superhuman doses. Well-known heroes and heroines of this genre include both real and imaginary legends. Davy Crockett and Annie Oakley both lived; fictional heroes include Pecos Bill and Paul Bunyan. Originally delivered in the oral tradition, tall tales feature exaggeration and hyperbole told as if it were the straight truth, creating a humorous effect. Although these stories feature outrageous happenings and larger-than-life characters, they are set within realistic parameters, highlighting the contrast between fact and fiction.

Book Links

Sally Ann Thunder Ann Whirlwind Crockett: A Tall Tale by Steven Kellogg (Morrow Junior Books, 1995)
From birth, Sally Ann surpassed her nine older brothers in the skills needed to master the wilderness. At the age of eight years old, she strikes off to face the frontier alone and, unaided, manages to skin a live bear and rescue Davy Crockett. This read-aloud picture book features delightfully humorous illustrations. Other tall tales by the same author include *Pecos Bill, Johnny Appleseed,* and *Mike Fink.*

A Million Fish . . . More or Less
by Patricia C. McKissack (Knopf, 1991)
In this read-aloud picture book, McKissack presents this classic "fish that got away" story, with Louisiana spirit. Hugh Thomas has been warned that Bayou Clapateaux is a peculiar place with strange goings on. With great confidence, he quickly catches a million fish. Can he hang on to them?

Teaching Tips

* Review the characteristics of tall tales with students. Discuss why the early settlers might have relished these tales and why they are still enjoyed today.

* Explain that hyperbole states the impossible. It is basically exaggerated exaggeration. For example, an exaggeration might be, "I was so tired, I could have slept for 20 hours." A hyperbole expressing the same idea might be, "I was so tired, I could have slept for 100 years." Ask students to create their own examples of hyperbole and exaggeration. Challenge them to express the same idea, first as an exaggeration and then as hyperbole.

* After students read a tall tale, invite them to write their own story starring this same hero or heroine. Ask students to consider how they will incorporate the character's superior skills or qualities into the events of their story.

The One That Got Away

Materials

photocopies of pages 44–46   pencils
scissors   glue
crayons or colored pencils

Teacher Directions

1. Review the genre definition with students. If time allows, share one or more of the book links (page 42) with students before starting the project.

2. Tell students that they are going to write their own tall tale. Discuss the following scenario:

Story Starter

The story begins in the early evening. Family and friends are gathered around the table when the main character and a companion return from a fishing trip empty-handed. They were supposed to catch fresh fish for dinner, but instead they arrive with a wild tale of how they almost caught the world's most amazing fish—an extraordinary, never-before-seen specimen! The main character narrates a series of events, describing how they nearly caught this fish through their own cleverness, courage, and perseverance. But, in the end, all they have to show for their efforts is their outrageous story of the one that got away.

3. Give students a copy of the prewriting page (page 44) and review the directions. Brainstorm and discuss possible responses for each of the questions. Show students a completed pop-up project for inspiration.

4. Have students complete the prewriting page, continuing on the back if needed. Encourage them to plan the beginning, middle, and end of their story and to use hyperbole. When students have finished planning, invite them to write a rough draft on a separate sheet of paper. Allow time for revision.

5. Give students copies of the pop-up page and cutouts (pages 45 and 46) and review the directions on page 46. Help students follow the directions to draw details on the cutouts and assemble the pop-up. Remind students to complete the pop-up based on the information from their prewriting page and story.

6. Have students write their final copy on the lines of the pop-up page, continuing on additional pages as needed. The finished project will show the two main characters in a canoe with speech balloons and a picture of the fish under the flap in the lake.

Extension Activity

Write a tall tale involving a different animal. Imagine that the main character and his or her friend are camping and they come across another extraordinary animal. How do they react? What exaggerated story do they bring home this time?

Name ______________________ Date ______________________

Prewriting Page

The One That Got Away

Complete this page to plan your tall tale. You may use the prompt below to begin.

My friend ______________________ and I returned from our fishing trip exhausted and empty-handed.
(friend's name)

Main Character's Name: ______________________

Description: ______________________

____

____

Friend's Name: ______________________

Description: ______________________

____

____

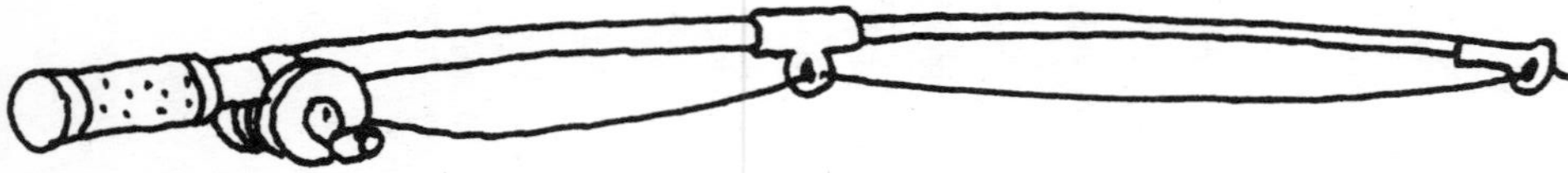

List the events that occurred as they tried to reel in the fish.

First, ______________________

____

Next, ______________________

____

Finally, ______________________

____

Describe the fish that got away.

____

____

____

____

____

The One That Got Away/Pop-Up

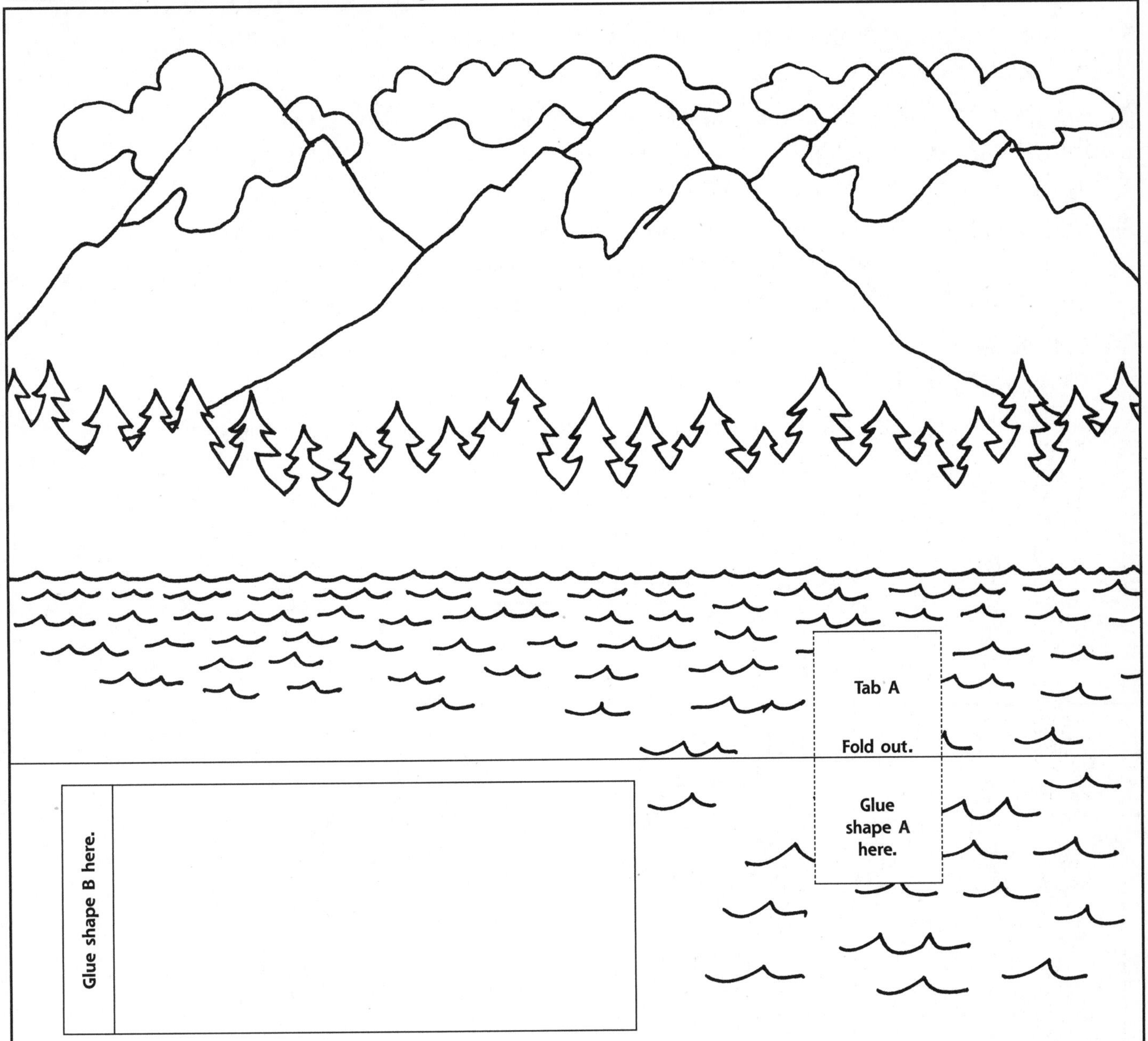
Tab A
Fold out.
Glue shape A here.
Glue shape B here.

Title: ______________________________

Author: ______________________________

The One That Got Away/Cutouts

1. On the pop-up, color the background. Draw the unusual fish from your story in the blank space. Cut out the page.

2. Fold the pop-up in half so the blank sides are touching. Cut the tab along the dotted lines. Fold the pop-up in half the other way, pushing in the tab and firmly creasing the tab on the fold line.

3. Draw details on the main character, the companion, and the boat (shape A). Fill in the speech balloons with exclamations that the characters say when they see the fish. Color the water flap (shape B). Cut out the shapes below.

4. Fold the water flap (shape B) forward along the fold line. Glue shape B to the space on the pop-up.

5. Glue the boat (shape A) to tab A on the pop-up, leaving room to open the flap.

Shape A—Characters and Boat

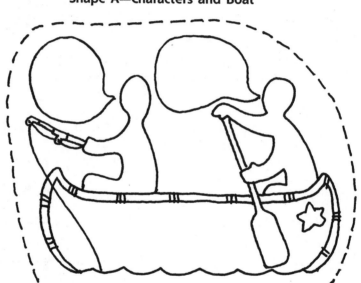

Shape B—Water Flap

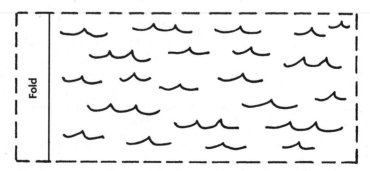

The Fastest Kid in the West

Materials

photocopies of pages 48–50
scissors
crayons or colored pencils

pencils
glue

Teacher Directions

1. Review the genre definition with students. If time allows, share one or more of the book links (page 42) with students before starting the project.

2. Tell students that they are going to write their own tall tale. Discuss the following scenario:

Story Starter

The story takes place out West—either in the present or during the time of the Wild West. The main character has just moved to town. He or she has a hidden talent that is soon discovered—amazing speed! The main character can run faster than the fastest runners in town, faster than a stone rolling down a mountain—even faster than a jackrabbit! How does the character put his or her extraordinary speed to use? Describe how the character uses his or her speed in everyday situations and then how it comes in handy to solve one major problem. Narrate the story from the point of view of another character.

3. Give students a copy of the prewriting page (page 48) and review the directions. Brainstorm and discuss possible responses for each of the questions. Show students a completed pop-up project for inspiration.

4. Have students complete the prewriting page, continuing on the back if needed. Encourage them to plan the problem and solution and to use hyperbole in their descriptions. When students have finished planning, invite them to write a rough draft on a separate sheet of paper. Allow time for revision.

5. Give students copies of the pop-up page and cutouts (pages 49 and 50) and review the directions on page 50. Help students follow the directions to draw details on the cutouts and assemble the pop-up. Remind students to complete the pop-up based on the information from their prewriting page and story.

6. Have students write their final copy on the lines of the pop-up page, continuing on additional pages as needed. The finished project will show the main character speeding along on a movable tab. Students draw details in the background to illustrate a part of the story, such as the climax.

Extension Activity

Write another tall tale in which the main character has a different extraordinary talent or skill. Perhaps the character can speak 20 languages fluently or play any instrument perfectly on the first try. How does the character use this talent? How does this skill help the character or others?

Name _____ Date _____

The Fastest Kid in the West

Complete this page to plan your tall tale. You may use the prompt below to begin.

When _____ moved to town, none of us suspected . . .
(main character)

Main Character's Name:

_____

Description:

_____

_____

Who is the narrator?

_____

What is the setting (time and place)?

_____

_____

Use hyperbole (extreme exaggeration) to describe the main character's speed. Write two descriptive sentences.

1. _____

_____

2. _____

_____

What is the main problem of the story?

_____

_____

_____

How does the main character use his or her speed to solve the problem?

_____

_____

_____

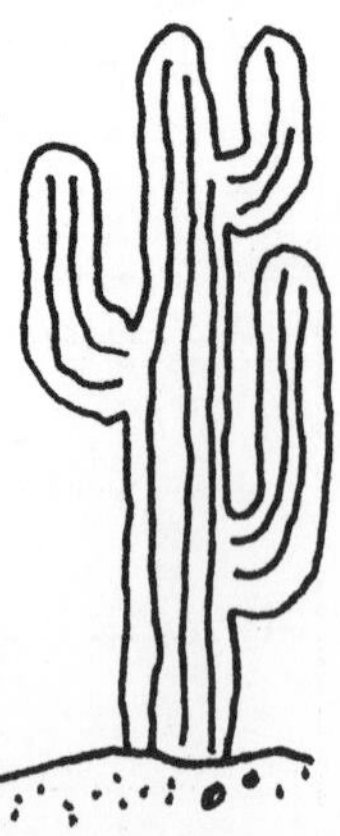

Tab A

Fold out.

Do not
glue.

Title: _____

Author: _____

_____

_____

_____

_____

_____

_____

The Fastest Kid in the West/Cutouts

1. On the pop-up, add details to show a part of your story. You might show how the main character uses his or her speed to solve the main problem. Cut out the page.

2. Fold the pop-up in half so the blank sides are touching. Cut the tab along the dotted lines. Fold the pop-up in half the other way, pushing in the tab and firmly creasing the tab on the fold line.

3. Draw details on the main character (shape A). Cut out shapes A and B below.

4. To make the main character slide across the pop-up, attach shape B to shape A as follows:

- Fold shape B forward along the fold lines. Do not fold shape A.

- Glue tab 1 on shape B to shape A.

- Thread the back strip through tab A on the pop-up.

- Glue tab 2 to connect the ends.
  NOTE: Do not glue shape A to tab A.

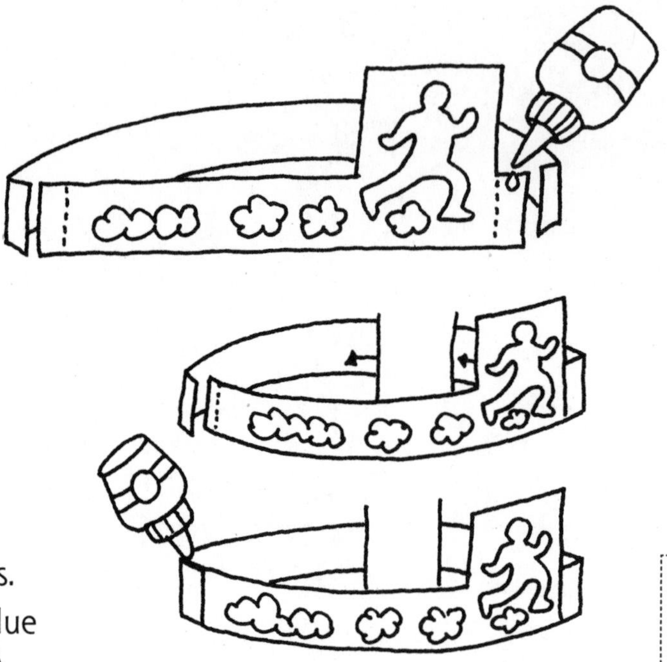

Shape A—Main Character

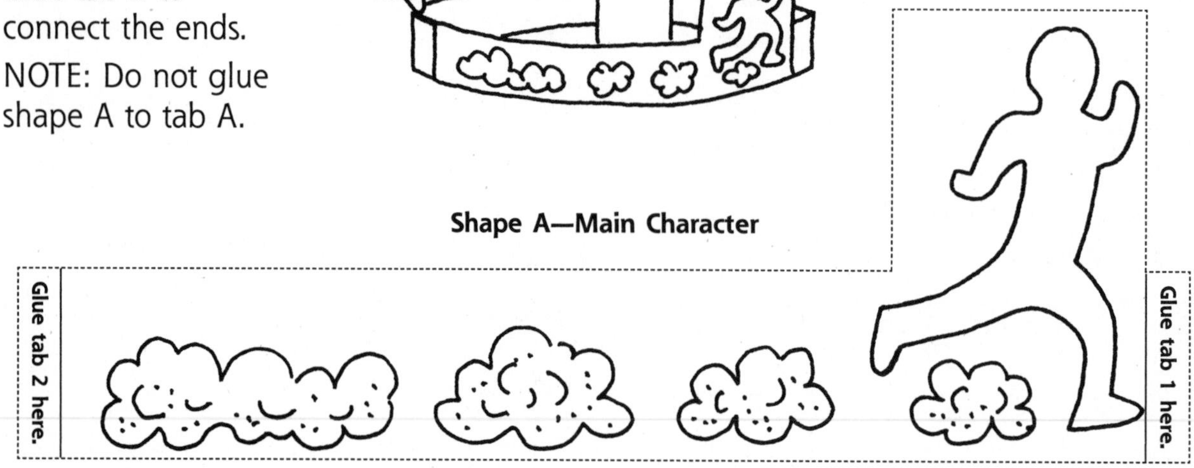

Glue tab 2 here.

Glue tab 1 here.

Shape B

Tab 2—Glue

Fold

Fold

Tab 1—Glue

FAIRY TALES

About the Genre

Part of the larger category of folktales, fairy tales were originally passed down through the generations as oral narrative. Fairy tales exist around the world, with different cultures sharing their own versions of similar stories. These tales are usually set in some nonspecific, "long ago" time and place and feature a cast of characters that includes elves, dragons, witches, trolls, goblins, talking animals, princes, and princesses. The main character often must solve a problem, perform a deed, or accomplish a goal. In the process, the character faces challenges and usually encounters an evil antagonist. Magic often plays a role in these stories as well, for example, in the form of a magical being who offers assistance to the main character. In the end, good overcomes evil. The main characters are rewarded for their good deeds and virtuous qualities and live happily ever after.

Book Links

Cinderella by K. Y. Craft
(SeaStar Books, 2000)
This delightful read-aloud is a grand retelling of the classic tale. It features elaborate illustrations and interesting details, such as the transformation of an injured bluebird, helped by Cinderella, into her fairy godmother.

A Frog Prince by Alix Berenzy
(H. Holt, 1989)
This beautifully illustrated read-aloud book tells the story of an enamored medieval frog pining for a princess. Once rejected by the princess, the endearing frog searches for a new love. On his quest, he faces and overcomes challenges and is rewarded for his courage and kindness. Told from the frog's point of view, this fairy tale truly entertains.

Teaching TiPS

* Begin with a discussion of favorite fairy tales. Together, make a list of the characteristics of the genre. What do these stories have in common?

* Share Cinderella stories from different regions of the world, such as *Yeh-Shen* by Ai-Ling Louie (China), *Cendrillon* by Robert D. San Souci (Caribbean), and *Kongi and Potgi* by Oki S. Han (Korea). Invite students to note the similarities and differences among the tales. Compare them to the retelling by K. Y. Craft (see Book Links).

* Challenge students to write fractured versions of classic fairy tales. Explain that a fractured tale takes the original story and makes it different in a bold and often humorous way. For example, they might write a modern-day Cinderella story in which Cinderella yearns to go to a ballpark instead of a ball.

The Three Wishes

Materials

photocopies of pages 53–55   scissors   craft sticks
8½- by 11-inch sturdy white paper   pencils
crayons or colored pencils   glue

Teacher Directions

1. Review the genre definition with students. If time allows, share one or more of the book links (page 51) with students before starting the project.

2. Tell students that they are going to write their own fairy tale. Discuss the following scenario:

Story Starter

The story begins long ago, deep in the heart of a faraway forest. The main character is walking through the forest gathering berries. He or she encounters a magical elf caught in a trap set by a wicked ogre who has taken off with the elf's pot of gold. The hero frees the elf from the trap, and in return, the elf promises to share his gold if the hero can assist him in getting it back. He grants the hero three wishes to use against the ogre's magical powers. How does the hero use these wishes to retrieve the gold?

3. Give students a copy of the prewriting page (page 53) and review the directions. Brainstorm and discuss possible responses for each of the questions. Show students a completed pop-up project for inspiration.

4. Have students complete the prewriting page, continuing on the back if needed. Encourage them to plan how the three wishes will lead the hero to the gold. When students have finished planning, invite them to write a rough draft on a separate sheet of paper. Allow time for revision.

5. Give students copies of the pop-up page and cutouts (pages 54 and 55) and review the directions on page 55. Either photocopy or mount the templates on sturdy paper or card stock. Help students follow the directions to draw details on the cutouts and assemble the pop-up. Remind students to complete the pop-up based on the information from their prewriting page and story.

6. Have students write their final copy on the lines of the pop-up page, continuing on additional pages as needed. The finished project will show a stagelike setting in the forest. Have students use their character puppets to act out a scene from their story for classmates.

(NOTE: As an alternative, have students create their pop-up project before they write their rough draft. Encourage students to use their puppets to generate ideas and dialogue for their stories. Invite them to work on their own or with a partner.)

Extension Activity

Retell the story from the ogre's point of view. What is his or her side of the story? How does the ogre feel about the elf? What does he or she do upon realizing that the main character has magic wishes to use in the quest to retrieve the gold?

Name _____ Date _____

The Three Wishes

Complete this page to plan your fairy tale. You may use the prompt below to begin.

Once upon a time in a tranquil forest far away, _____
(main character)
was gathering berries when suddenly he/she heard a squeal coming from behind a bush.

Main Character's Name:
_____

Description:
_____
_____
_____
_____

Elf's Name:
_____

Description:
_____
_____
_____
_____

Ogre's Name:
_____

Description:
_____
_____
_____
_____

List the main character's three wishes.

How does each wish help retrieve the gold?

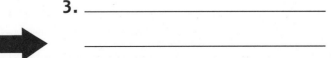

1. _____
_____
_____

1. _____
_____
_____

2. _____
_____

2. _____
_____

3. _____
_____

3. _____
_____

Tab A

Fold out.

Glue left side of shape A here.

Tab B

Fold out.

Glue right side of shape A here.

Title: _____

Author: _____

_____

_____

_____

_____

_____

_____

The Three Wishes/Cutouts

Note: Photocopy or mount the pop-up and cut-outs on sturdy paper or card stock.

1. On the pop-up, color the background. Cut out the page.

2. Fold the pop-up in half so the blank sides are touching. Cut the tabs along the dotted lines. Fold the pop-up in half the other way, pushing in the tabs and firmly creasing the tabs on the fold line.

3. Color the trees (shape A). Draw the main character, the elf, and the ogre on shapes B, C, and D to create puppets. Cut out the shapes below. Tape a craft stick to the back of each puppet.

4. Glue the left tree trunk (shape A) to tab A on the pop-up. Glue the right trunk to tab B.

5. Move your puppets on the pop-up "stage" to act out the events in your story.

Shape A—Trees

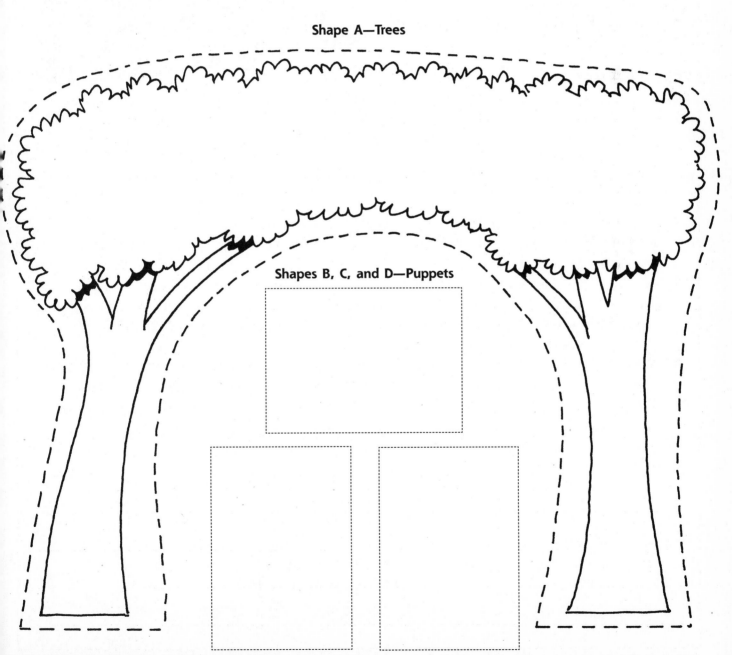

Shapes B, C, and D—Puppets

Magic in a Sack

Materials

photocopies of pages 57–59
scissors
crayons or colored pencils

pencils
glue

Teacher Directions

1. Review the genre definition with students. If time allows, share one or more of the book links (page 51) with students before starting the project.

2. Tell students that they are going to write their own fairy tale. Discuss the following scenario:

Story Starter

The story begins outside the walls of an enormous castle. The main character is pondering how to get inside to rescue his or her friend who has been captured by a wicked queen. A good fairy has taken pity on the main character and has supplied a sack containing magical objects that will help in the rescue. Unfortunately, the queen has cast three spells designed to thwart the rescue. How does the main character use the magical objects to overcome the spells and complete the rescue mission successfully? What becomes of the wicked queen?

3. Give students a copy of the prewriting page (page 57) and review the directions. Brainstorm and discuss possible responses for each of the questions. Show students a completed pop-up project for inspiration.

4. Have students complete the prewriting page, continuing on the back if needed. Encourage them to plan how each magical object helps the main character overcome one of the queen's spells. When students have finished planning, invite them to write a rough draft on a separate sheet of paper. Allow time for revision.

5. Give students copies of the pop-up page and cutouts (pages 58 and 59) and review the directions on page 59. Help students follow the directions to draw details on the cutouts and assemble the pop-up. Remind students to complete the pop-up based on the information from their prewriting page and story.

6. Have students write their final copy on the lines of the pop-up page, continuing on additional pages as needed. The finished project will show the magical objects on a flap behind the sack as well as an important event inside the castle.

Extension Activity

What if the good fairy had not come along to assist the main character? Could the character rescue his or her friend using wits alone? Write a tale that describes such a rescue attempt. Without magic, does it seem like a fairy tale?

Name _____ Date _____

Magic in a Sack

Complete this page to plan your fairy tale. You may use the prompt below to begin.

"These castle walls must be three feet thick and fifty feet high! How will I get inside to rescue my friend from the wicked queen?" wondered _____.

(main character)

Main Character's Name:

_____

Description:

_____

_____

Friend's Name:

_____

Description:

_____

_____

Queen's Name:

_____

Description:

_____

_____

List the three magic spells the queen casts to prevent the main character from rescuing his/her friend.

What objects are in the sack?

_____

How do these objects help overcome the spells?

1. _____

_____

_____

 1. _____

_____

_____

2. _____

_____

 2. _____

_____

3. _____

_____

 3. _____

_____

Glue shape B here.

Tab A

Fold out.

Glue shape A here.

Title: _____

Author: _____

_____

_____

_____

_____

_____

Magic in a Sack/Cutouts

1. On the pop-up, draw an important event from your story inside the castle. Color the background. Cut out the page.

2. Fold the pop-up in half so the blank sides are touching. Cut the tab along the dotted lines. Fold the pop-up in half the other way, pushing in the tab and firmly creasing the tab on the fold line.

3. Color the outside of the castle (shape B) and the magic sack (shape A). Draw the magical objects on the flap behind the sack. Cut out the shapes below.

4. Fold the sack (shape A) back along the fold line. Glue the sack to tab A on the pop-up.

5. Fold the castle (shape B) forward along the fold line. Glue the castle to the pop-up.

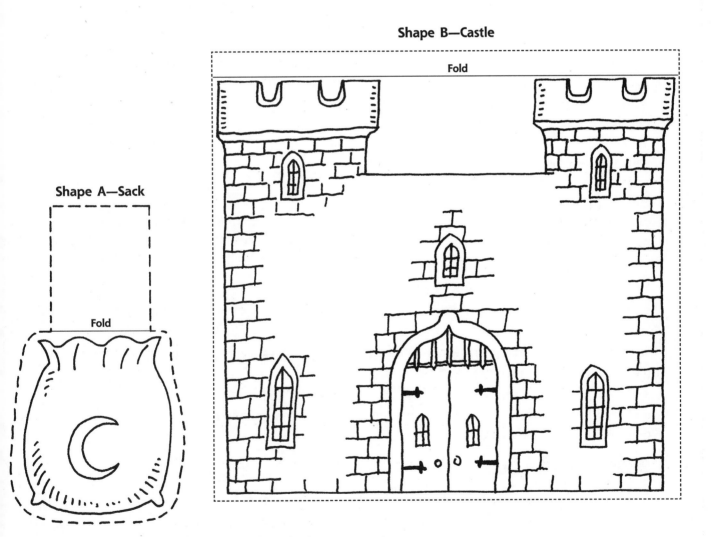

Shape B—Castle

Fold

Shape A—Sack

Fold

HISTORICAL FICTION

About the Genre

Writers of historical fiction conduct extensive research in order to have a thorough understanding of the time period in which their story is set. In historical fiction, fictitious yet realistic characters are placed in a historically authentic situation. Some of the characters encountered in historical fiction may actually have lived. The setting of these stories is a definite time and place in history, and the characters experience events that could have occurred in this setting. They express themselves through realistic dialogue, thought, and action. Well-written historical fiction allows readers to empathize with the characters and become involved in the story, while also providing them with a sense of a particular chapter in history.

Book Links

I'm Sorry, Almira Ann by Jane Kurtz
(Holt, 1999)
This chapter book presents eight-year-old Sarah and her friend Almira Ann as they tackle ordeals faced by pioneers on the Oregon Trail.

A Journey to the New World: The Diary of Remember Patience Whipple, Mayflower, 1620
(Dear America Series) by Kathryn Lasky (Scholastic, 1996)
This book is part of a series of books that combine historical fiction with the genre of journals and diaries. Twelve-year-old Mem recounts the hardships faced by the Pilgrims on their two-month journey aboard the *Mayflower*.

Resources for Research

If You Traveled West in a Covered Wagon by Ellen Levine (Scholastic, 1992)
This nonfiction book provides lively details of everyday life on the Oregon Trail.

Samuel Eaton's Day: A Day in the Life of a Pilgrim Boy by Kate Waters (Scholastic, 1989)
This read-aloud picture book features full-color photos depicting a day in the life of Samuel Eaton, a 17th-century child living on Plimoth Plantation.

Teaching Tips

* Brainstorm a list of questions students have about the time period in which they are going to set their stories. Have students consult books, Web sites, and other reference materials to find the answers.

* Divide the class into small groups. Have each group create informative visual presentations on specific topics about a historical period. Topics might include food, clothing, medicine, transportation, recreation, and so on. Students can then use this information in their story.

* Visit these and other Web sites for information about Pilgrims and the Oregon Trail.

  Plimoth Plantation: **www.plimoth.org**
  Pilgrim Hall Museum: **www.pilgrimhall.org**
  Oregon Trail: **http://www.isu.edu/ %7Etrinmich/Oregontrail.html**

The Ship Has Arrived!

Materials

photocopies of pages 62–64
scissors
crayons or colored pencils

pencils
glue

Teacher Directions

1. Review the genre definition with students. If time allows, share one or more of the historical fiction book links (page 60) with students before starting the project.

2. Tell students that they are going to write their own piece of historical fiction. Discuss the following scenario:

Story Starter

The story takes place in Plymouth, Massachusetts in the 1620s. The first Pilgrims that settled in Plymouth brought supplies, but they relied on ships from Europe to supplement and replace the items they used or wore out. Ships carrying goods arrived infrequently, however, and families had to make do with what they had originally brought. When a ship did arrive, the goods were distributed among the families. After researching Pilgrim life, write about a family's day-to-day existence before the arrival of a specific item. What problems does the family face without this item? How do they manage? Then describe the arrival of the ship. What item does the ship bring for the family and how does it improve their lives?

3. Give students a copy of the prewriting page (page 62) and review the directions. Brainstorm and discuss possible responses for each of the questions. You might provide suggestions for the desired item, such as tools, pots, and so on. Show students a completed pop-up project for inspiration.

4. Have students complete the prewriting page, continuing on the back if needed. Encourage them to plan how the family's life is affected by the lack of a particular item and how it is improved by having this item. When students have finished planning, invite them to write a rough draft on a separate sheet of paper. Allow time for revision.

5. Give students copies of the pop-up page and cutouts (pages 63 and 64) and review the directions on page 64. Help students follow the directions to draw details on the cutouts and assemble the pop-up. Remind students to complete the pop-up based on the information from their prewriting page and story.

6. Have students write their final copy on the lines on the pop-up page, continuing on additional pages as needed. The finished project will show a large pop-up ship. Students draw the desired item under a flap in the ship's hold.

Extension Activity

Write a diary entry of one of the characters in the story. Describe an event in the story from this character's point of view. Include additional details by telling how the main character spent his or her day. What kind of chores did he or she do? What did the character do for entertainment?

The Ship Has Arrived!

Complete this page to plan your piece of historical fiction. You may use the prompt below to begin your story.

_____ 's mother sighed and said, "Winter will be coming before
(main character)
long. How I hope a ship will arrive soon! Perhaps it will have _____
(name of object)
that we so badly need."

Main Character

Name and Description

_____
_____
_____
_____
_____
_____

Other Family Members

Names and Descriptions

_____
_____
_____
_____
_____
_____

What item does the Pilgrim family need?

_____

What problems do they face as a result of not having this item?

_____
_____

How do they cope with these problems?

_____
_____

How does this item help the Pilgrim family?

_____
_____
_____
_____

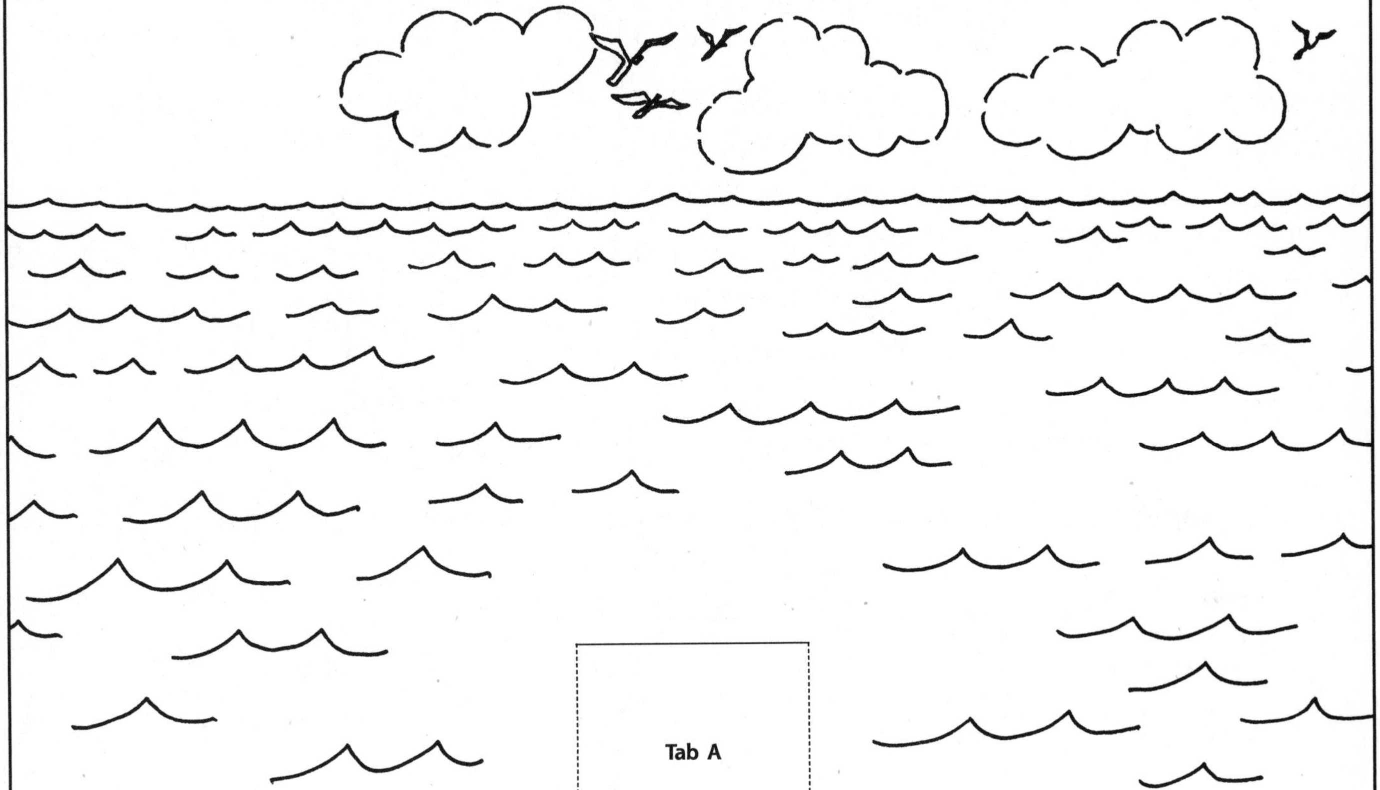

Tab A

Fold out.

Glue shape A here.

Title: _____

Author: _____

_____

_____

_____

_____

_____

1. On the pop-up, color the background. Cut out the page. Fold the pop-up in half so the blank sides are touching. Cut the tab along the dotted lines. Fold the pop-up in half the other way, pushing in the tab and firmly creasing the tab on the fold line.

2. Draw the desired item from your story in the space on the ship (shape A). Color the ship. Color the flap (shape B) the same color as the ship. Cut out the shapes below.

3. Fold the flap (shape B) forward along the fold line. Glue the flap to the ship (shape A). Glue the ship to tab A on the pop-up.

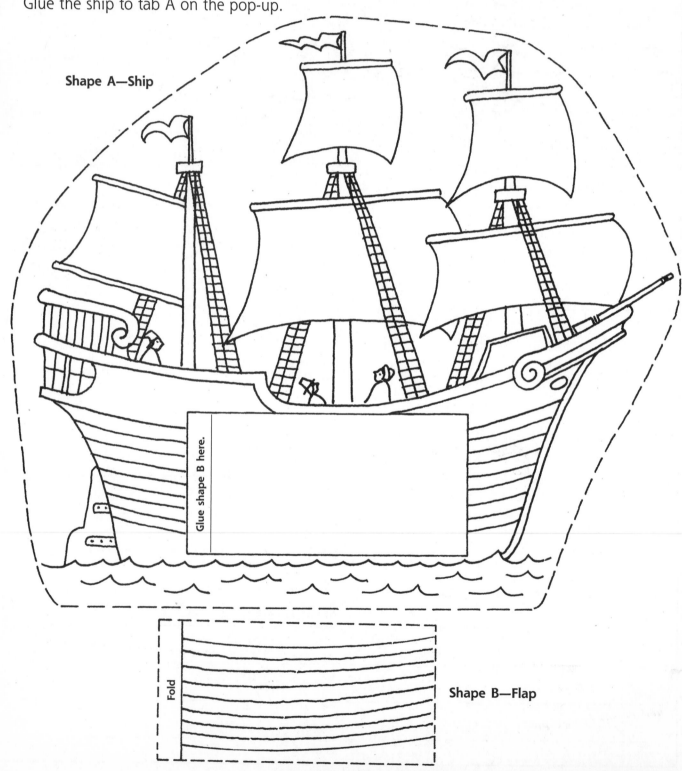

Shape A—Ship

Glue shape B here.

Fold

Shape B—Flap

On the Oregon Trail

Materials

photocopies of pages 66–68
scissors
crayons or colored pencils

pencils
glue

Teacher Directions

1. Review the genre definition with students. If time allows, share one or more of the historical fiction book links (page 60) with students before starting the project.

2. Tell students that they are going to write their own piece of historical fiction. Discuss the following scenario:

Story Starter

The story begins on the Oregon Trail in the 1840s. The main character—a pioneer child—and his or her family have been traveling for two months and have a long way to go before they reach their destination. On their travels, the main character comes across a stick with a slit cut into it stuck in the ground. Inside is a message written on a scrap of paper that was left by a previous group of pioneers. The message warns the pioneer group about a challenge ahead. This could be crossing a river, hunting buffalo, getting stuck in the mud, or dealing with another problem. What does the message say? How do the pioneers tackle the problem ahead? In your story, include lots of details about what it was like to travel on the Oregon Trail.

3. Give students a copy of the prewriting page (page 66) and review the directions. Brainstorm and discuss possible responses for each of the questions. Show students a completed pop-up project for inspiration.

4. Have students complete the prewriting page, continuing on the back if needed. Encourage them to plan how the problem will be resolved. When students have finished planning, invite them to write a rough draft on a separate sheet of paper. Allow time for revision.

5. Give students copies of the pop-up page and cutouts (pages 67 and 68) and review the directions on page 68. Help students follow the directions to draw details on the cutouts and assemble the pop-up. Remind students to complete the pop-up based on the information from their prewriting page and story.

6. Have students write their final copy on the lines on the pop-up page, continuing on additional pages as needed. The finished project will show a large prairie schooner and a pop-up of the main character holding the message found on the trail. Students draw the inside of the prairie schooner under the flap.

Extension Activity

Pioneers could leave letters at some forts, where they would be picked up by another wagon train and carried home. Write a letter from the main character in the story to someone in their hometown describing an event in the story. Include authentic pioneer vocabulary and details about the food they ate, games they played, and chores they performed in order to survive.

Name _____

Date _____

On the Oregon Trail

Complete this page to plan your piece of historical fiction. You may use the prompt below to begin your story.

"Look, a message!" _____ shouted and ran toward the stick stuck in the ground by the side of the trail.
(main character)

What does the message say?

_____
_____
_____
_____
_____

Main Character's Name: _____

Description: _____
_____
_____

Family Members' Names and Descriptions: _____
_____
_____
_____
_____

What details can you include about life on the Oregon Trail?

_____
_____
_____
_____

How do they deal with the problem?

_____
_____
_____

What problem do the pioneers face?

_____
_____
_____

Glue shape C here.

Tab A

Fold out.

Glue shape A or B here.

Title: _____

Author: _____

_____

_____

_____

_____

_____

_____

On the Oregon Trail/Cutouts

1. On the pop-up, draw the inside of the prairie schooner and color the background. Cut out the page.

2. Fold the pop-up in half so the blank sides are touching. Cut the tab along the dotted lines. Fold the pop-up in half the other way, pushing in the tab and firmly creasing the tab on the fold line.

3. Choose either shape A for a girl or shape B for a boy. Draw details on the main character. Write the message found on the trail in the rectangle. Cut out the shapes below.

4. Glue shape A or B to tab A on the pop-up.

5. Fold the prairie schooner flap (shape C) forward along the fold line. Glue the flap to the prairie schooner on the pop-up.

Shape A—Pioneer Girl　　　　　　　　　　**Shape B—Pioneer Boy**

Shape C—Prairie Schooner Flap

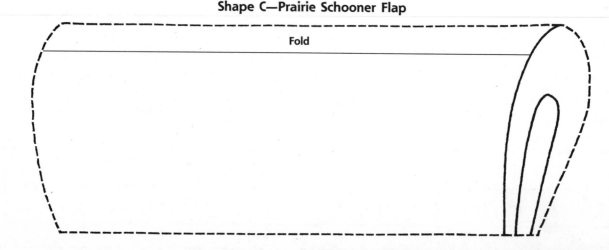

Fold

PERSONAL NARRATIVE

About the Genre

In a personal narrative, the author recounts in the first person a real experience from his or her life. Authors of this nonfiction genre usually describe not only an event that they experienced, but also their emotional responses to it, revealing why this particular event held meaning for them. These stories follow a narrative sequence and elaborate on significant details that illuminate the point of the story. The tone of a personal narrative reflects the author's personality and is appropriate for the subject of the story. Through sensory descriptions and precise language, the author strives to make readers feel that they are experiencing the events of the story.

Book Links

Childtimes: A Three-Generation Memoir by Eloise Greenfield and Lessie Jones Little (Crowell, 1979) A grandmother, mother, and daughter share poignant childhood memoirs, spanning the 1880s to the 1950s. Photographs and drawings complement the text.

26 Fairmount Avenue by Tomie dePaola (G. P. Putnam's Sons, 1999) In this easy-to-read chapter book, dePaola recounts events from his childhood with engaging details and a light touch of humor. A Newbery Honor book.

When I Was Nine by James Stevenson (Greenwillow Books, 1986) This picture book combines beautiful illustrations and crisp language to portray a summer of the author's life in the 1930s.

Teaching TIPS

* Invite students to make a time line of a year in their lives. Challenge them to consider carefully which events to include. You might make a time line of a year in your childhood to provide a model. Have students discuss the events on their time lines and choose one as the subject for a personal narrative.

* Create a bulletin board of interesting facts from the memoirs the class will be reading without identifying the source or speaker. Use these facts to spark interest in and discussion about the books.

* Have students either bring photographs from home (with family's permission) or draw pictures of events from their past. Encourage them to use these as inspiration for personal narrative writing assignments.

What I Treasure Most

Materials

photocopies of pages 71–73   pencils
scissors   glue
crayons or colored pencils

Teacher Directions

1. Review the genre definition with students. If time allows, share one or more of the book links (page 69) with students before starting the project. You might choose sections to read aloud.

2. Tell students that they are going to write their own personal narrative that they will share with the class. Discuss the following assignment:

Story Starter

What do you treasure most in the world? These treasures could be anything—think beyond objects. You might include people, animals, or special skills or qualities that you possess. After making a list of your treasures, choose something from your list that has an interesting story behind it. It could be something you lost and then found again, something gained through hard work, or something that was a surprise. Or you might relate a story about a person or animal that is special to you. In your narrative, make sure to show rather than tell why you value this treasure. Remember that the purpose of the piece is to share something about yourself with your readers, and perhaps discover something about yourself in the process.

3. Give students a copy of the prewriting page (page 71) and review the directions. Brainstorm and discuss possible responses for each of the questions. Show students a completed pop-up project for inspiration.

4. Have students complete the prewriting page, continuing on the back if needed. Encourage them to think about which details will help strengthen the piece and clarify the focus. When students have finished planning, invite them to write a rough draft on a separate sheet of paper. Allow time for revision.

5. Give students copies of the pop-up page and cutouts (pages 72 and 73) and review the directions on page 73. Help students follow the directions to draw details on the cutouts and assemble the pop-up. Remind students to complete the pop-up based on the information from their prewriting page and narrative.

6. Have students write their final copy on the lines of the pop-up page, continuing on additional pages as needed. The finished project will show the student standing beside a large treasure chest. Inside the chest, students draw their treasure. (Note: If students write about a person or animal, they might create a pop-up of this person or animal in place of the treasure chest. If they write about a quality or skill, they can draw a picture that represents it.)

Extension Activity

Write about something you treasured as a young child. It could be anything—an imaginary friend, a blanket, a favorite place. What was it and why was it so important to you? What memories do you have of it? How did this treasure make you feel and why? Do you still cherish this treasure or have your feelings changed?

What I Treasure Most

Complete this page to plan your personal narrative. You may use the prompt below to begin.

When I think about what I treasure, what stands out is . . .

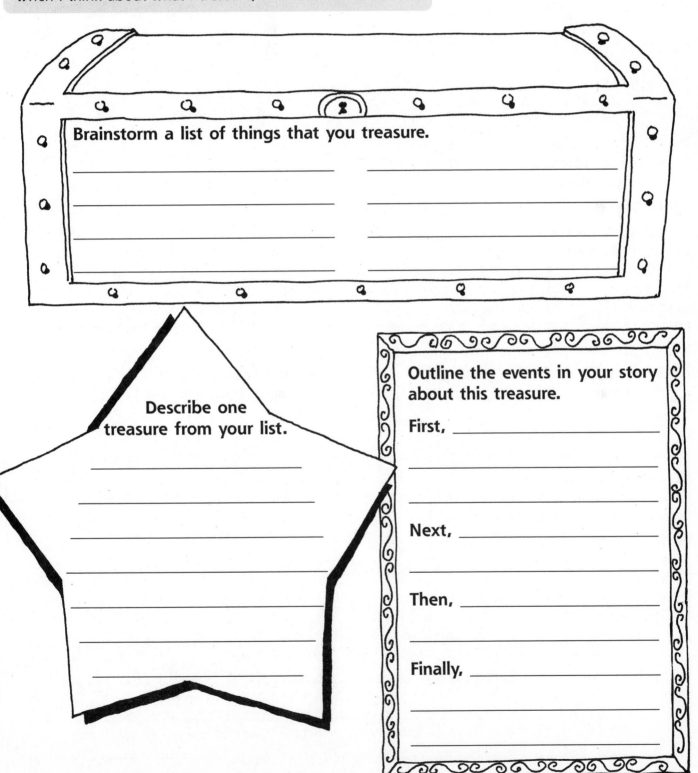

Brainstorm a list of things that you treasure.

**Describe one
treasure from your list.**

**Outline the events in your story
about this treasure.**

First, _____

_____

Next, _____

_____

Then, _____

_____

Finally, _____

_____

What I Treasure Most

Tab A

Fold out.

Glue
shape A
here.

Tab B

Fold out.

Glue
shape B
here.

Title: _____

Author: _____

_____

_____

_____

_____

_____

_____

What I Treasure Most/Cutouts

1. On the pop-up, color the background any way you like. Cut out the page.

2. Fold the pop-up in half so the blank sides are touching. Cut the tabs along the dotted lines. Fold the pop-up in half the other way, pushing in the tabs and firmly creasing the tabs on the fold line.

3. Draw the thing you treasure in the treasure chest (shape B). Color the flap (shape C). Draw details on your self-portrait (shape A). Cut out the shapes below.

4. Fold shape C forward along the fold line. Glue shape C to the chest (shape B). Glue the chest to tab B on the pop-up.

5. Glue the self-portrait (shape A) to tab A on the pop-up.

Shape A—Self-Portrait

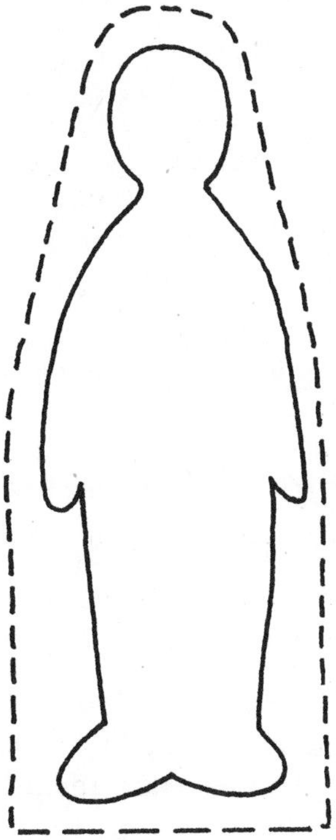

Shape B—Treasure Chest

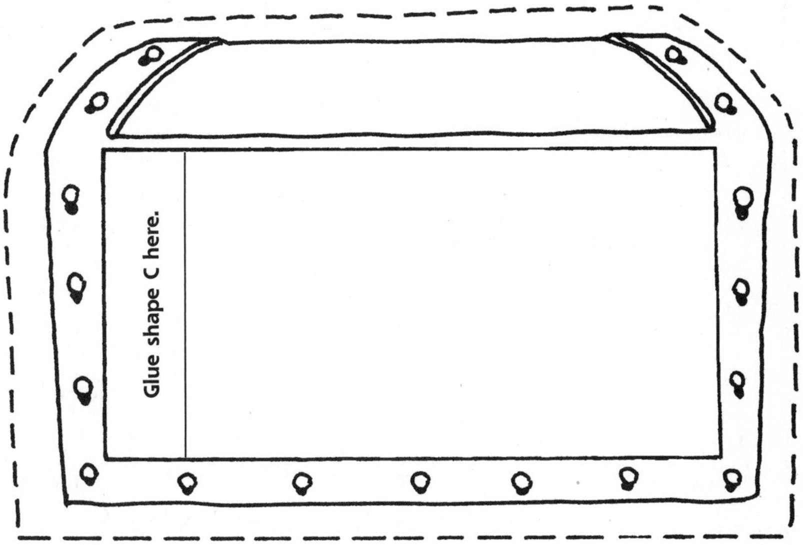

Glue shape C here.

Shape C—Flap

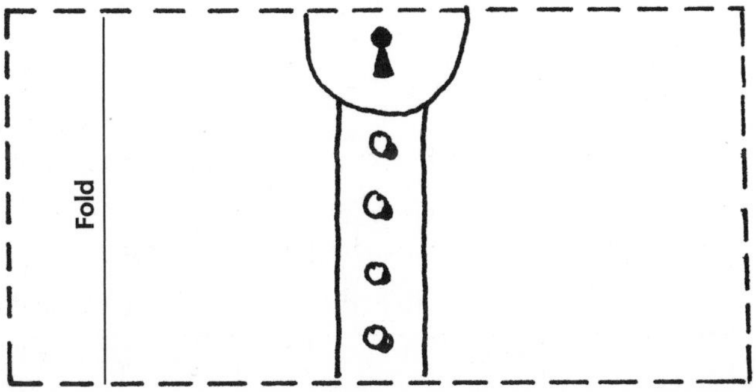

Fold

Who Am I?

Materials

photocopies of pages 75–77   pencils
scissors   glue
crayons or colored pencils

Teacher Directions

1. Review the genre definition with students. If time allows, share one or more of the book links (page 69) with students before starting the project. You might choose sections to read aloud.

2. Tell students that they are going to write their own personal narrative. Discuss the following assignment:

Story Starter

Think about the important experiences you have had. It could be a time you accomplished something, traveled somewhere, overcame a fear, learned from a mistake, or acquired a new skill. Choose one experience that lends itself to an interesting story that includes dialogue, description, and action. Think about why this experience was important. What did you learn about yourself, others, or the world? As you are writing your narrative, be sure to include a beginning, middle, and end. There's one catch: Do not reveal any information that would give away your identity. Let your classmates try to guess whose story it is, based on the information provided.

3. Give students a copy of the prewriting page (page 75) and review the directions. Brainstorm and discuss possible responses for each of the questions. Show students a completed pop-up project for inspiration.

4. Have students complete the prewriting page, continuing on the back if needed. Encourage them to plan the beginning, middle, and ending of their narrative. When students have finished planning, invite them to write a rough draft on a separate sheet of paper. Allow time for revision.

5. Give students copies of the pop-up page and cutouts (pages 76 and 77) and review the directions on page 77. Help students follow the directions to draw details on the cutout and assemble the pop-up. Remind students to complete the pop-up based on the information from their prewriting page and story.

6. Have students write their final copy on the lines of the pop-up page, continuing on additional pages as needed. The finished project will show a drawing of the student with a flap covering the face so that the student's identity remains hidden. In the background, students draw something related to their story in the picture frame.

Extension Activity

Often, it's the everyday occurrences—rather than special events—that can reveal the most about a person. What is something you do as part of your daily or weekly routine that shows something important about yourself? Write a personal narrative describing one particular time you took part in this activity and what it reveals about you.

Name _____

Date _____

Who Am I?

Complete this page to plan your personal narrative. You may use the prompt below to begin.

Who am I? Take a guess after you've read this story about me.

What is the topic of your personal narrative?

_____

_____

What does this narrative tell about you? Why is this important?

_____

_____

First,

Next,

Then,

Finally,

Tab A

Fold out.

Glue
shape A
here.

Title: _____

_____

_____

_____

_____

_____

_____

1. In the frame on the pop-up, draw something important related to your story, such as the main event. Cut out the page.

2. Fold the pop-up in half so the blank sides are touching. Cut the tab along the dotted lines. Fold the pop-up in half the other way, pushing in the tab and firmly creasing the tab on the fold line.

3. Draw details on your self-portrait (shape A). Cut out the shape.

4. Fold shape A forward along the fold line so the circle covers the face. Draw a question mark on the outside of the circle.

5. Glue the self-portrait (shape A) to tab A on the pop-up.

Shape A—Self-Portrait

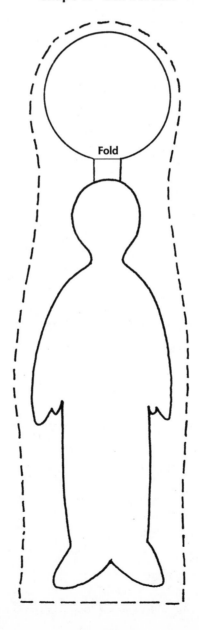

Fold

EXPOSITORY WRITING

About the Genre

Expository writing presents and explains information to the reader and can take many forms, such as directions, book reports, essays, and newspaper articles. Expository writing should have a clear main idea that is supported by facts, descriptions, explanations, and examples. It should be geared toward a specific audience and organized in a logical way that facilitates the reader's understanding of the subject. It may also include graphs, diagrams, maps, tables, illustrations, photographs, or other graphic aids to complement the text and extend the reader's understanding. The activities in this section challenge students to write a newspaper article and an informational report. These forms of writing call for writers to research and report up-to-date information on a particular subject. In these pieces, writers address the who, what, where, when, how, and why of a subject in an interesting and informative way.

Book Links

The Egyptian News by Scott Steedman (Candlewick Press, 1997)
Students will enjoy reading this fun historical account of ancient Egypt in which everyday activities and historical events are vividly described in a newspaper format.

What a Great Idea! Inventions That Changed the World by Stephen M. Tomecek (Scholastic, 2003) This informative and visually pleasing resource groups together inventions into five main time periods. Tomecek describes each invention and how it influenced civilization in easy-to-understand language.

Teaching Tips

* Review the above genre definition with students. Ask students to think about the many sources of expository information they come across in their day-to-day lives, such as newspaper and magazine articles, Web sites, brochures, encyclopedias, and so on.

* Show students examples of graphic aids from books and magazines. Then challenge them to create graphic aids to present classroom information, such as how to put away books, care for classroom pets, use the computer, and so on.

* Choose an age-appropriate news article for students to read and analyze prior to writing the School News article (page 79). Ask students to underline the information in the article that answers the questions *Who? What? Where? When? How? and Why?*

School News

Materials

photocopies of pages 80–82   pencils
scissors   glue
crayons or colored pencils

Teacher Directions

1. Review the genre definition with students. If time allows, share one or more of the book links (page 78) with students, as well as several newspaper articles, before starting the project. Discuss the features of an article, such as the headline, lead, body of the article, photos, and captions.

2. Tell students that they are going to write their piece of expository writing in the form of a newspaper article about a real school event. As a class or in small groups, brainstorm a list of newsworthy school events. Then discuss the following assignment:

Story Starter

Imagine that you are a newspaper reporter sent to your school to cover newsworthy events. Choose one event for the front page of the newspaper. Write a catchy headline (or title) for the article. Then write a lead (or first sentence) that gives the reader the basic facts. In your article, answer the big questions: *Who? What? Where? When? How?* and *Why?* Be sure to make your article rich and informative with interesting details and quotations.

3. Give students a copy of the prewriting page (page 80) and review the directions. Brainstorm and discuss possible responses for each of the questions. Show students a completed pop-up project for inspiration.

4. Have students complete the prewriting page, continuing on the back if needed. When they have finished planning, invite them to write a rough draft on a separate sheet of paper. Encourage students to write in the style of a newspaper reporter. Allow time for revision.

5. Give students copies of the pop-up page and cutouts (pages 81 and 82) and review the directions on page 82. Help students follow the directions to draw details on the cutouts and assemble the pop-up. Remind students to complete the pop-up based on the information from their prewriting page and article.

6. Have students write their final copy on the lines of the pop-up page, continuing on additional pages as needed. The finished project will show three photographs related to the article with captions.

Extension Activity

Write a newspaper article covering an event that happened outside of school. It could be something that happened in your own life, a recent event in the news, or an event from history. (Research the event, if needed.) Remember to answer the six big questions and include a headline and lead.

School News

Complete this page to plan your article.

Hot Off the Press!

Headline (a catchy title): _____

_____

Lead (first sentence that tells the basic facts):

_____

_____

Answer the six big questions with important details.

Who? _____

_____

What? _____

_____

Where? _____

_____

When? _____

_____

How? _____

_____

Why? _____

_____

Glue the bottom right corner of the **first** picture here.

Extra! Extra!
Read all about it!

Glue the bottom left corner of the **second** picture here.

Glue the bottom center of the **third** picture on the tab below.

Tab C

Fold out.

Glue third picture here.

Title: _____

Author: _____

_____

_____

_____

_____

_____

School News/Cutouts

1. On the pop-up, color the background any way you like. Cut out the page.

2. Fold the pop-up in half so the blank sides are touching. Cut the tab along the dotted lines. Fold the pop-up in half the other way, pushing in the tab and firmly creasing the tab on the fold line.

3. In shapes A, B, and C, draw pictures that show the sequence of events of your news article. Write a brief caption below each picture. Cut out the shapes below.

4. Glue shapes A and B to the corners of the pop-up so that they extend off the pop-up. Glue shape C to tab C on the pop-up.

Shape A—First Picture　　　　　　　　　**Shape B—Second Picture**

1st

2nd

3rd

Shape C—Third Picture

My Favorite Invention

Materials

photocopies of pages 84–86   pencils
scissors   glue
crayons or colored pencils

Teacher Directions

1. Review the genre definition with students. If time allows, share one or more of the book links (page 78) with students before starting the project.

2. Tell students that they are going to write an informational report about their favorite invention. As a class, generate a list of favorite inventions and ask students to provide reasons for their choices. (See page 78 for a reference book.) Then discuss the following assignment:

Story Starter

Choose your all-time favorite invention as the subject of your report. First, you'll need to find out all about it. Research the invention and gather all the facts. The purpose of your report is to inform your reader about the invention. In it, you'll answer the questions *Who? Where? When? How?* and *Why?* Notice that you will not be answering the question *What?* As you are writing your report, be sure not to name the invention. Let your classmates read the report and guess the invention from the information provided.

3. Give students a copy of the prewriting page (page 84) and review the directions. Brainstorm and discuss possible responses for each of the questions. Show students a completed pop-up project for inspiration.

4. Have students complete the prewriting page, continuing on the back if needed. When students have finished planning, invite them to write a rough draft on a separate sheet of paper. Encourage students to think of creative ways to refer to their invention without giving it away. Allow time for revision.

5. Give students copies of the pop-up page and cutouts (pages 85 and 86) and review the directions on page 86. Help students follow the directions to assemble the pop-up. Remind students to complete the pop-up based on the information from their prewriting page and story.

6. Have students write their final copy on the lines of the pop-up page, continuing on additional pages as needed. The finished project will show three clues about the invention on a sliding panel and a drawing of the invention behind the panel. After students have read the clues and guessed the invention, they can slide the panel to see if they were correct.

Extension Activity

Choose a different topic as the subject of an informational report, such as a place, sport, or famous person. Create a K-W-L chart by drawing three columns. In the first column (K), write what you already *know* about this topic. In the second column (W), write what you *want to know* about it. After researching your topic, write what you *learned* in the third column (L). Organize your information into categories and then write your report on the topic.

Name _____ Date _____

My Favorite Invention

Complete this page to plan your informational report. You may use the prompt below to begin.

My all-time favorite invention _____.

(State the invention's purpose without revealing its name.)

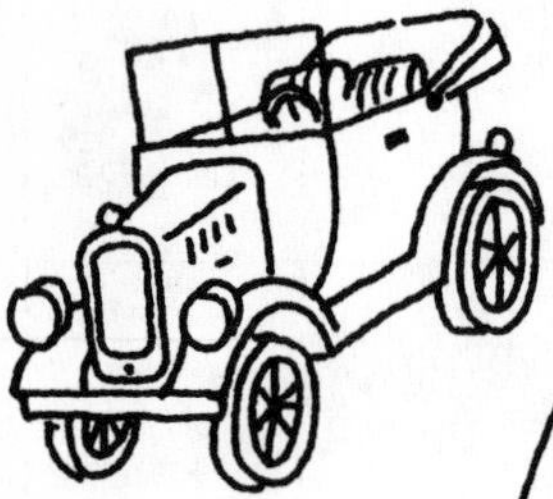

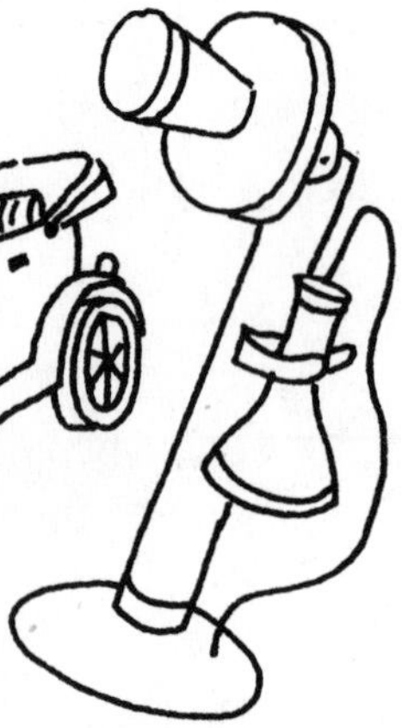

What was invented?

_____

_____

_____

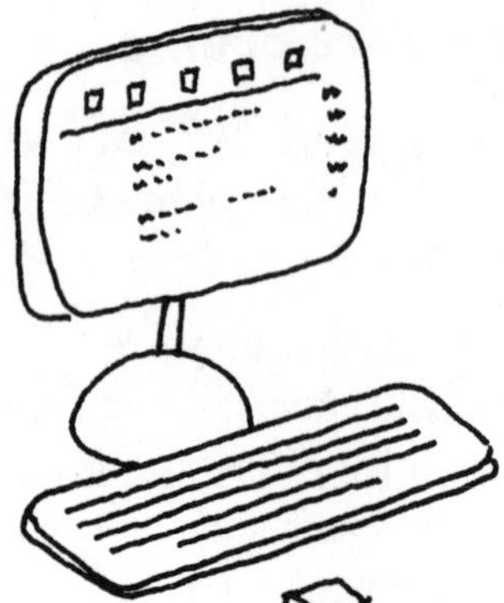

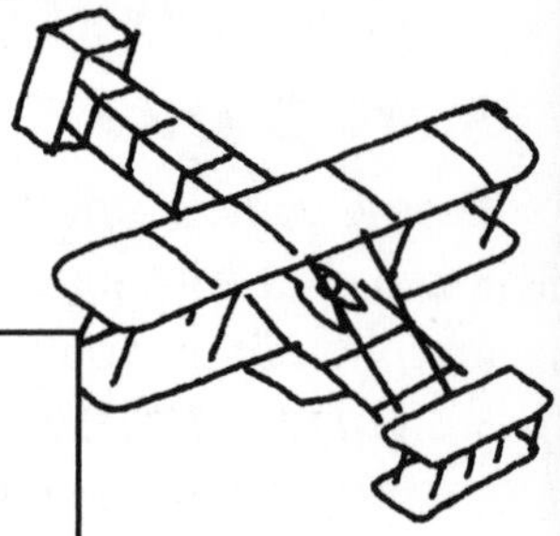

Who was the inventor?

_____

_____

_____

When was it invented?

_____

_____

_____

Where was it invented?

_____

_____

_____

How was it invented?

_____

_____

_____

Why was it invented?

_____

_____

_____

Guess the Invention!

Tab A

Fold out.

Do not
glue.

Title: _____

Author: _____

_____

_____

_____

_____

_____

My Favorite Invention/Cutouts

1. On the pop-up, draw your favorite invention in the space. Color the background and cut out the page.

2. Fold the pop-up in half so the blank sides are touching. Cut the tab along the dotted lines. Fold the pop-up in half the other way, pushing in the tab and firmly creasing the tab on the fold line.

3. Write three clues about the invention on shape A. Color and cut out the shapes A and B below.

4. To make a sliding panel, attach shape B to shape A as follows:

- Fold shape B forward along the fold lines.

- Place shape A on top of shape B. Glue tab 1 (shape B) to shape A.

- Thread the back strip through tab A on the pop-up.

- Glue tab 2 (shape B) to shape A. NOTE: Do not glue the panel to tab A.

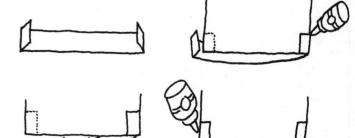

Shape A—Clues

Clues

1. _____

_____

2. _____

_____

3. _____

_____

Glue tab 2 here.

Glue tab 1 here.

Shape B

Tab 2   Fold   Fold   Tab 1

ADVENTURE

About the Genre

Packed with action and excitement, adventure stories typically depict a main character who must bravely face a challenge in nature or society. Often this challenge poses a threat to someone or something's well-being. The situation calls for the protagonist's strongest characteristics to surface, which aids him or her in achieving a specific goal. In this form of realistic fiction, the protagonist rises to the occasion and meets a challenge head-on, largely unassisted by others.

Book Links

Island of the Blue Dolphins
by Scott O'Dell
(Houghton Mifflin, 1960)
In this Newbery Medal winner, a young girl is stranded on an island for years, waiting to be rescued. Based on a true story, this captivating tale of survival describes how twelve-year-old Karana acquires food, clothing, and shelter—and how she ultimately discovers a sense of peace in her solitude.

Stone Fox
by John Reynolds Gardiner
(Crowell, 1980)
Ten-year-old Willy is determined to keep the family farm running. He stakes everything on the hope of winning the big prize money in a dogsled race against the legendary Stone Fox.

Teaching Tips

* Bring in travel brochures that feature faraway destinations, exotic settings, and exciting activities. Have students use these to help them brainstorm ideas for action-packed adventure stories.

* As a class, brainstorm a list of challenges people might face, and have students take a class vote for the challenge they will write about. Then have each student compile a supply list of five items they would like to have under their selected circumstances. For a series of five days, have students write a journal about their experiences. You might add a daily teacher-selected twist in their adventure for them to respond to. For example, if they are stranded on a desert island, day one could bring a rainstorm; day two, a wild animal eats the food supply; day three, a ship is spotted on the horizon; day four, the character is injured; and day five, a grove of coconut trees is located.

On Top of Mount Pinnacle

Materials

photocopies of pages 89–91   pencils
scissors   glue
crayons or colored pencils

Teacher Directions

1. Review the genre definition with students. If time allows, share one or more of the book links (page 87) with students before starting the project.

2. Tell students that they are going to write their own adventure story. Discuss the following scenario:

Story Starter

The story begins at the foot of the fictional Mount Pinnacle, a towering mountain that challenges only the most adventurous climbers to ascend its snowy peak. The main character and his or her friend have been training to climb Mount Pinnacle for a year and are finally ready for the expedition. Together they make the long, arduous ascent, only to find a surprise awaiting them at the top. What is the surprise at the top of the mountain? What challenges does it pose? How do the climbers deal with the surprise and safely descend the mountain?

3. Give students a copy of the prewriting page (page 89) and review the directions. Brainstorm and discuss possible responses for each of the questions. Show children a completed pop-up project for inspiration.

4. Have students complete the prewriting page, continuing on the back if needed. Encourage them to plan the climax and resolution of their story. When students have finished planning, invite them to write a rough draft on a separate sheet of paper. Allow time for revision.

5. Give students copies of the pop-up page and cutouts (pages 90 and 91) and review the directions on page 91. Help students follow the directions to draw details on the cutouts and assemble the pop-up. Remind students to complete the pop-up based on the information from their prewriting page and story.

6. Have students write their final copy on the lines of the pop-up page, continuing on additional pages as needed. The finished project shows the main character on a movable tab climbing Mount Pinnacle. On a flap behind the mountain, students draw the surprise waiting for the climbers at the top.

Extension Activity

Challenge yourself by thinking of a different climax for your story. How could the events have taken a different turn? Rewrite the story from the climax to the conclusion. How did the change of events affect the outcome of the story?

On Top of Mount Pinnacle

Complete this page to plan your adventure story. You may use the prompt below to begin.

_____ gazed up at Mount Pinnacle with its snowy peak beckoning him/her to rise to the challenge.

(main character)

Main Character's Name: _____

Description: _____

_____

Friend's Name: _____

Description: _____

_____

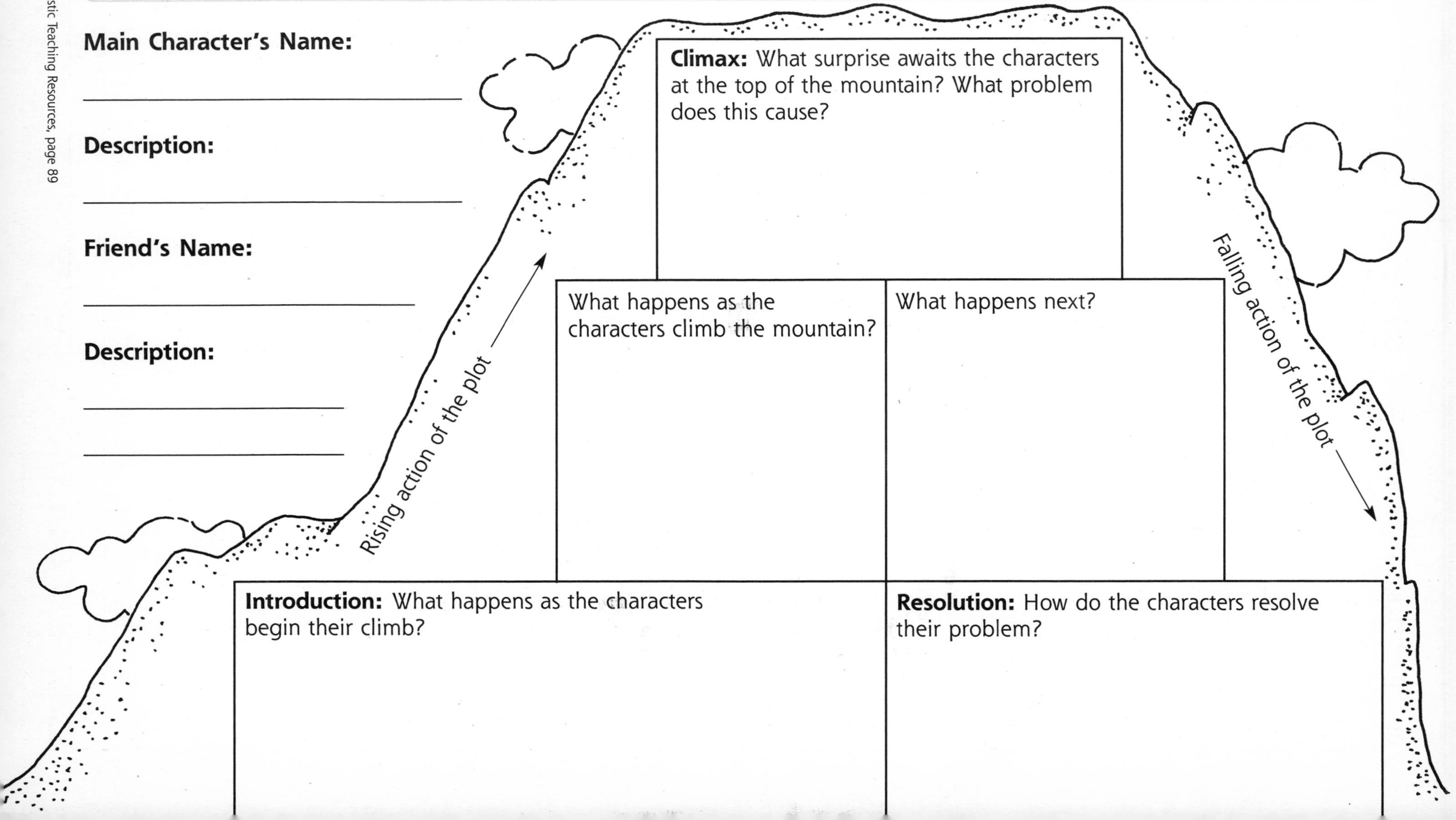

Introduction: What happens as the characters begin their climb?

Rising action of the plot

What happens as the characters climb the mountain?

What happens next?

Climax: What surprise awaits the characters at the top of the mountain? What problem does this cause?

Falling action of the plot

Resolution: How do the characters resolve their problem?

On Top of Mount Pinnacle/Pop-Up

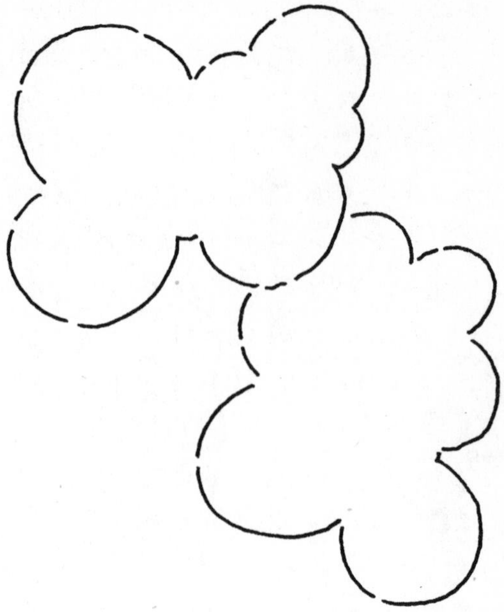

Glue top of shape C here.

Glue bottom of shape C here.

Tab A

Fold out.

Glue shape A here.

Title: ______________________________

Author: ______________________________

____

____

____

____

____

____

1. On the pop-up, color the background and cut out the page.

2. Fold the pop-up in half so the blank sides are touching. Cut the tab along the dotted lines. Fold the pop-up in half the other way, pushing in the tab and firmly creasing the tab on the fold line.

3. Draw details on the main character climbing the mountain (shape B). Color the mountain (shape A). On the flap, draw the surprise on top of the mountain. Cut out the shapes below.

4. Fold shape C as shown. Glue shape C to the boxes on the pop-up.

5. Fold the climber (shape B) back along the fold lines. Thread the strip behind shape C on the pop-up. Then glue the end of the strip to the back of shape B with a small dab of glue. NOTE: Do not glue the strip to shape C.

6. Fold the mountain (shape A) back along the fold line. Glue the mountain to tab A on the pop-up.

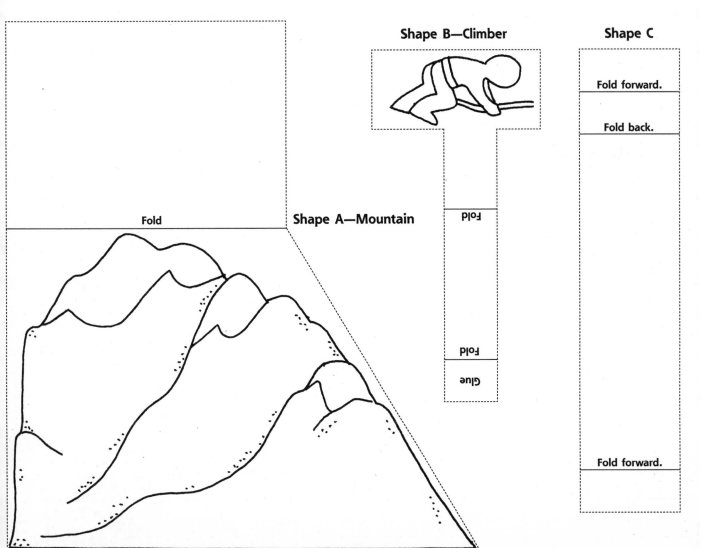

Fold

Shape A—Mountain

Shape B—Climber

Fold

Fold

Glue

Shape C

Fold forward.

Fold back.

Fold forward.

Maya Surprise

Materials

photocopies of pages 93–95   pencils
scissors   glue
crayons or colored pencils

Teacher Directions

1. Review the genre definition with students. If time allows, share one or more of the book links (page 87) with students before starting the project.

2. Tell students that they are going to write their own adventure story. Discuss the following scenario:

Story Starter

The scene is a fictional Maya temple in the Yucatán. The main character and a friend are visiting the Yucatán with a tour group. At the ancient Templo Maya, the character is intrigued by the tour guide's words: "Legend has it that the Templo Maya holds a secret that will be revealed only on the full moon in the Maya month of Yaxkin. That is tonight." That night, the main character and the friend sneak away and visit the ruins to see if they can find any clues to the secrets it holds. When they open a large stone door, they end up coming face-to-face with a secret. Students write about the ensuing adventure that takes place before the characters make their way safely back to the rest of the group.

3. Give students a copy of the prewriting page (page 93) and review the directions. Brainstorm and discuss possible responses for each of the questions. Show students a completed pop-up project for inspiration.

4. Have students complete the prewriting page, continuing on the back if needed. Encourage them to plan the climax and resolution of their story. When students have finished planning, invite them to write a rough draft on a separate sheet of paper. Allow time for revision.

5. Give students copies of the pop-up page and cutouts (pages 94 and 95) and review the directions on page 95. Help students follow the directions to draw details on the cutouts and assemble the pop-up. Remind students to complete the pop-up based on the information from their prewriting page and story.

6. Have students write their final copy on the lines of the pop-up page, continuing on additional pages as needed. The finished project will show the Templo Maya and its secret behind the sliding panel.

Extension Activity

Imagine that you are an archaeologist uncovering ancient ruins and you come across an amazing discovery that leads you on an action-packed adventure. Where does it take you? What happens on this adventure? How does it end?

Maya Surprise

Complete this page to plan your adventure story. You may use the prompt below to begin.

"Legend has it," our tour guide explained, "that the Templo Maya holds a secret that will be revealed only on the full moon in the Maya month of Yaxkin. That is tonight."

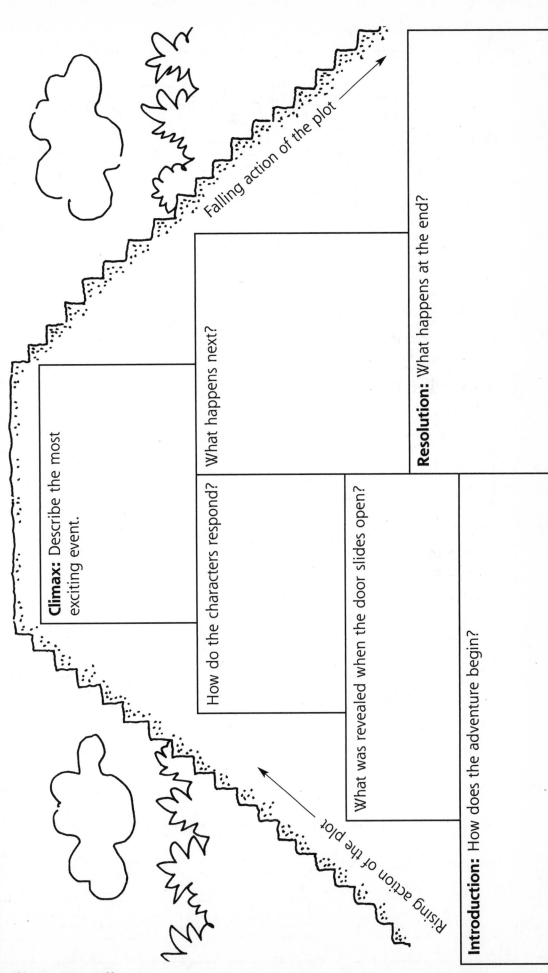

Falling action of the plot

Climax: Describe the most exciting event.

What happens next?

How do the characters respond?

What was revealed when the door slides open?

Resolution: What happens at the end?

Introduction: How does the adventure begin?

Rising action of the plot

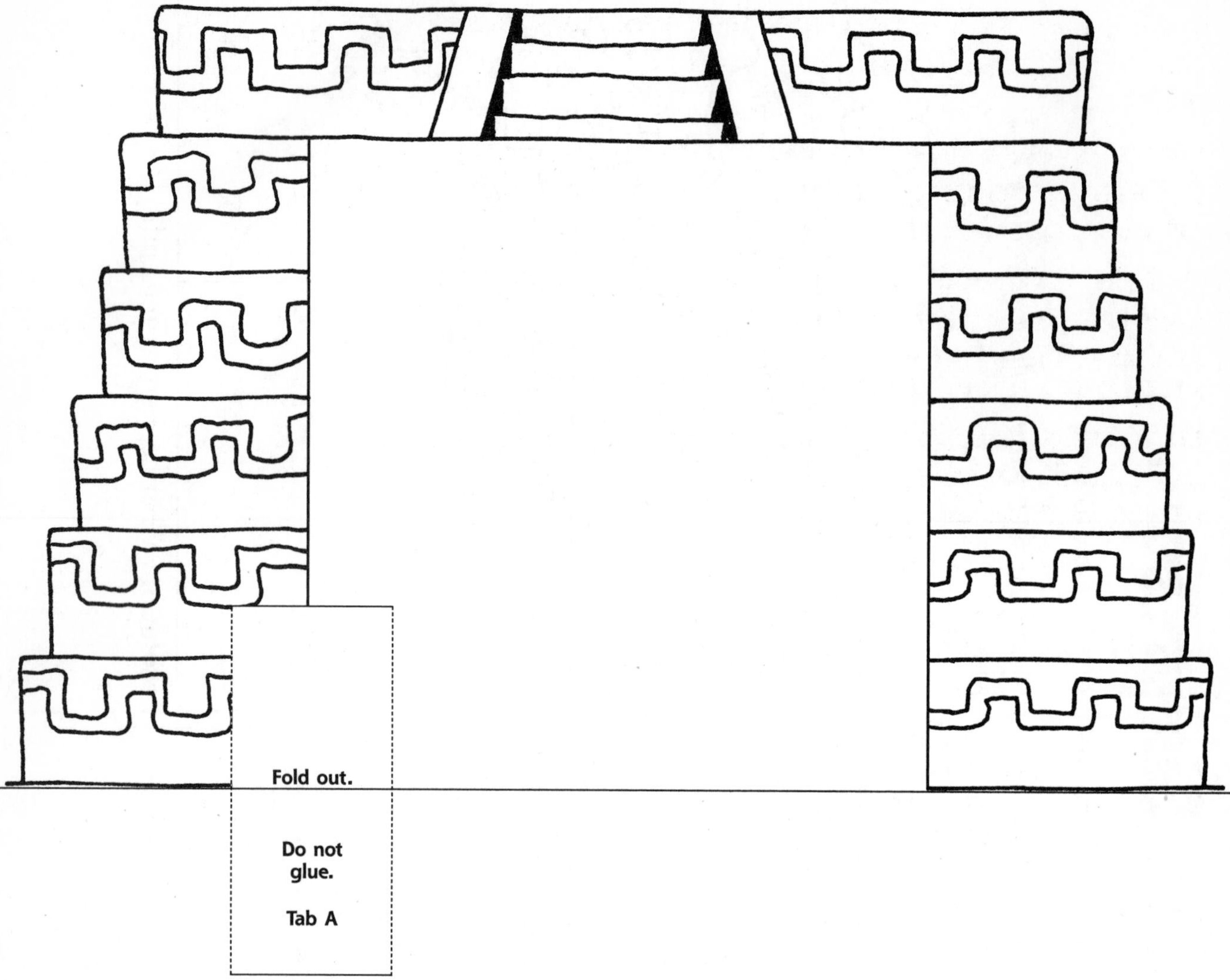

Fold out.

Do not glue.

Tab A

Title: _____

Author: _____

_____

_____

_____

_____

_____

1. In the square on the pop-up, draw the secret discovered inside the Templo Maya. Color the temple and background and cut out the page.

2. Fold the pop-up in half so the blank sides are touching. Cut the tab along the dotted lines. Fold the pop-up in half the other way, pushing in the tab and firmly creasing the tab on the fold line.

3. Color and cut out the sliding door (shape A). Fold back along the fold lines. Thread the strip behind tab A on the pop-up. Then glue the end of the strip to the back of shape A with a small dab of glue. NOTE: Do not glue shape A to tab A.

Glue

Fold

Shape A—Sliding Door

Fold

Resources

Cassidy, Janet. (2003). *Teaching Genre: Mysteries*. New York: Scholastic.

Clayton, Heather. (2003). *Great Genre Writing Lessons*. New York: Scholastic.

Fiderer, Adele. (1999). *40 Rubrics and Checklists*. New York: Scholastic.

Holmes, Kenneth L. (1983). *Covered Wagon Women: Diaries and Letters From the Western Trails, 1840–1849*. Glendale, CA: A. H. Clark Co.

Levine, Ellen. (1992). . . . *If You Traveled West in a Covered Wagon*. Scholastic.

McCarthy, Tara. (1998). *Expository Writing*. New York: Scholastic.

——. (1998). *Narrative Writing*. New York: Scholastic.

——. (1996). *Teaching Genre*. New York: Scholastic.

——. (2001). *Teaching Genre: Historical Fiction*. New York: Scholastic.

——. (2001). *Teaching Genre: Humorous Fiction*. New York: Scholastic.

——. (2001). *Teaching Genre: Science Fiction*. New York: Scholastic.

——. (2001). *Teaching Genre: Tall Tales*. New York: Scholastic.

McGovern, Ann. (1969). . . . *If You Sailed on the Mayflower in 1620*. Scholastic.

Miller, Marcia. (2000). *The Big Book of Ready-to-Go Writing Lessons*. New York: Scholastic.

Miller, Tamara B. (2001). *Pop-Up Discoveries*. Fearon Teacher Aids.

Volz, Bridget Dealy. (2000). *Junior Genreflecting: A Guide to Good Reads and Series Fiction for Children*. Englewood, CO: Libraries Unlimited.